Marius

ANCIENTS IN ACTION

Boudicca
Marguerite Johnson

Catiline
Barbara Levick

Catullus
Amanda Hurley

Cleopatra
Susan Walker and Sally-Ann Ashton

Hadrian
James Morwood

Hannibal
Robert Garland

Horace
Philip D. Hills

Lucretius
John Godwin

Martial
Peter Howell

Ovid: Love Songs
Genevieve Lively

Ovid: Myth and Metamorphosis
Sarah Annes Brown

Pindar
Anne Pippin Burnett

Sappho
Marguerite Johnson

Spartacus
Theresa Urbainszyk

Tacitus
Rhiannon Ash

Marius

Federico Santangelo

Bloomsbury Academic
An imprint of Bloomsbury Publishing Plc

B L O O M S B U R Y
LONDON • NEW DELHI • NEW YORK • SYDNEY

Bloomsbury Academic

An imprint of Bloomsbury Publishing Plc

50 Bedford Square	1385 Broadway
London	New York
WC1B 3DP	NY 10018
UK	USA

www.bloomsbury.com

BLOOMSBURY and the Diana logo are trademarks of Bloomsbury Publishing Plc

First published 2016

British Library Cataloguing-in-Publication Data
A catalogue record for this book is available from the British Library.

ISBN: PB: 978-1-47421-471-1
ePDF: 978-1-47421-473-5
ePub: 978-1-47421-472-8

Library of Congress Cataloging-in-Publication Data
Santangelo, Federico.
Marius / Federico Santangelo.
pages cm.– (Ancients in action)
An introduction to Marius– Why Marius matters– Marius' background– The context– Marius' rise– Marius' early career– The Jugurthine War– The Germanic War– Marius' fall– The wrong crowd– Elder statesman– Twists of fate– The Social War– Disruption and tradition : the first march on Rome–Marius' flight– The final comeback– Marius' legacy– The Mariani– Caesar and Cicero– Marius under the Principate.
Includes bibliographical references and index.
ISBN 978-1-4742-1471-1 (pb)– ISBN 978-1-4742-1472-8 (epub)– ISBN 978-1-4742-1473-5 (epdf) 1. Marius, Gaius, approximately 157 B.C.-86 B.C. 2. Statesmen--Rome–Biography. 3. Rome–History–Republic, 265-30 B.C. 4. Rome–History, Military–265-30 B.C. I. Title.
DG256.5.S46 2015
937.05092–dc23
[B]
2015019277

Series: Ancients in Action

Typeset by Fakenham Prepress Solutions, Fakenham, Norfolk NR21 8NN
Printed and bound in India

per Giovanni Geraci

Contents

Acknowledgements

I am very grateful to Alan Beale and Roger Rees for inviting me to write this book, and am especially indebted to Roger for offering me some crucial advice on *how* to write it. I am also very grateful to the anonymous readers who commented on a proposal and an early draft. One of them also generously shared with me the stemma of the Marii that I am including in the text (p. 13). Fiona Noble, Antonio Pistellato, Lorna Rimell, and Alexander Thein offered invaluable advice on various drafts. Ryan Horne at the Ancient World Mapping Center (University of North Carolina, Chapel Hill) provided helpful cartographical guidance and support. I am grateful to the Center for permission to reproduce the map that is printed on p. xii. At Bloomsbury Charlotte Loveridge, Anna MacDiarmid and Alice Reid expertly guided me throughout the various stages of the project. Kim Storry at Fakenham Prepress Solutions oversaw the production of the volume.

This book stems from teaching, and sets out to be used primarily (though by no means exclusively) in the classroom. My foremost debt is therefore to the several cohorts of Newcastle students with whom I have been discussing Marian matters over the years, and whose reactions to some of the arguments presented here have deeply informed my thinking on the period and my choices on how to frame this account.

The dedication is a small token of gratitude and affection to a scholar and teacher from whom I have learned a great deal more than I could possibly say.

Chronology
(all dates BC)

103	Third consulship of Marius. Agrarian bill of the tribune Saturninus.
102	Fourth consulship. Major Roman victory against the Teutones at Aquae Sextiae.
101	Fifth consulship. Decisive victory against the Cimbri at Vercellae (July). Tribunate of Glaucia.
100	Sixth consulship. Tribunate of Saturninus. Assassination of Nonius. New agrarian bill. Tensions with the Senate. 10 December: *senatus consultum ultimum*. Death of Saturninus and Glaucia.
98	Marius' trip to Asia Minor. Election to the augurate.
97	Marius returns to Rome.
95	*Lex Licinia Mucia*; case of T. Matrinius.
91	Tribunate of M. Livius Drusus; citizenship bill; outbreak of the Social War.
90	Marius is active on the northern front of the war (central Italy) under the consul P. Rutilius Lupus.
89	Marius withdraws from the operations.
88	Consulship of Sulla; tribunate of Sulpicius. Controversy over the Mithridatic command. Riots in Rome; Marius is assigned the command. Sulla's troops march on the city. Marius is declared a public enemy and is compelled to flee Rome.
87	Marius escapes to North Africa. In Rome, clash between Cn. Octavius and L. Cornelius Cinna. Marius returns to Italy and joins forces with Cinna. March on Rome and ensuring massacre. December: Marius and Cinna are elected to the consulship.
86	Mid-January: Marius dies, probably of natural

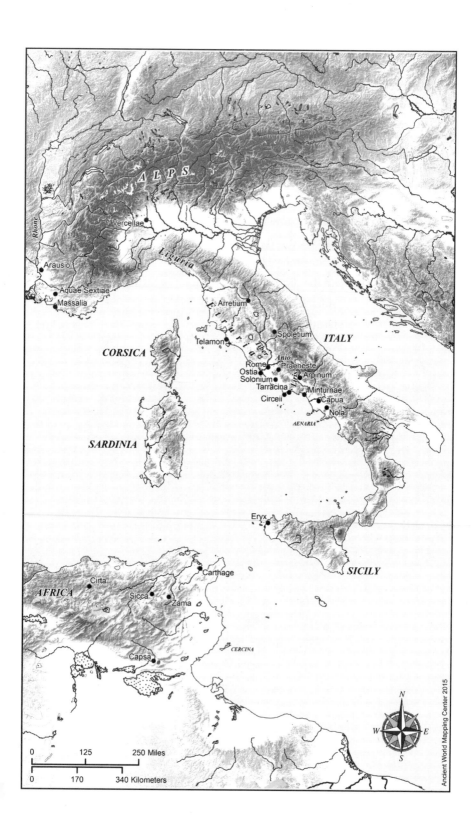

An Introduction to Marius

Why Marius matters

The most authoritative and influential works on the history of the late Roman Republic over the last half century or so have tended to focus on wide-ranging processes, on long-term developments in some key areas, and on the role of some social groups. To be sure, plenty of substantial studies have been produced on the part that a number of major figures – from the Gracchi to Sulla, Cicero, and Caesar – had in political developments, but mostly with a view to offering a more precise understanding of how the initiatives and policies of some individuals were affected by, and impacted on, wider historical trends. 'Great Man' history is not in favour – and rightly so.

This book is certainly not an attempt to redress the balance in the opposite direction. It is, first and foremost, an attempt to sketch an account of the life and career of Gaius Marius. It tries to do so by setting Marius in context and by asking the wider question of what aspects of short-term discontinuity and long-term change he intro-duced. There are many widely known aspects of Marius' biography that set him apart as a remarkable figure in Roman history, and as one that announces new times, as the Republic is heading towards an age of disruption. He was an exceptionally successful individual, who obtained the consulship on seven occasions, in spite of hailing from a family that had never produced a senator before him; a commander who appears to have introduced new methods of recruitment in the Roman army and established a remarkable bond with his men; a military leader who saved Italy from a major threat from the north; a political leader who joined forces with ruthless allies to pass a range of reforms that were intended more to provide his soldiers with land than to bring relief to the poor; an elder statesman who was first compelled to flee Rome when his main opponent (and former aide) marched on the city at the helm of an army, and then launched a spectacular comeback, followed by a round of unprecedented massacres, only to die (probably of natural causes) two weeks into his seventh consulship.

At several points in his life Marius achieved a level of power and influence that was virtually unprecedented; he was revered by the people of Rome and supported by the crowd of his veterans. The great German historian Theodor Mommsen (1817–1903) argued that Marius intended to establish a system of personal rule, and indeed came very close to achieving it. At the same time, he claimed, like many other scholars, that Marius was politically inept, and that he failed to gather sufficient consensus and obtain lasting political results, in spite of the magnitude of his military achievements and the prestige that they had conferred upon him. Recent discussions of the period have gone some way to showing that this is a reductive view. It is beyond doubt that Marius faced a number of considerable political setbacks, but his political longevity and the resilience with which he remained a force to be reckoned with for decades, throughout a highly volatile political context, should induce one to adopt a more generous assessment of his talents in the Forum and on the Senate floor, as well as on the battlefield.

More generally, and more importantly, Marius is a figure through whom some levels of major historical change may be identified and understood. It is fair to say that his lifetime ranged across a period through which the Roman Republic changed beyond recognition; in the second part of his life, he was one of the major movers of that process of change. The way in which his career unfolded points to a scenario in which the time-honoured checks and balances through which political competition had functioned in Rome were going through a crisis: Marius' seven consulships were a symptom, not the cause of a far-reaching development. The wars in which he was involved mark the consolidation of the Roman hegemony across the Mediterranean world, as well as the expansion of the Roman citizen body, following the enfranchisement of the Italian Allies. The makeup of the Roman armies also went through considerable change, and came to include increasing numbers of poor soldiers, especially from the countryside. The bond between soldiers and commanders became increasingly strong, especially as the prospect of substantial war booty became attractive to those who had much to gain from the material rewards that victory could generate. Those trends were already firmly entrenched within the historical trajectory of the Republic by the mid-second century BC, and Marius engaged with them in an original and highly effective fashion.

Indeed, the view that the relationship and balance between army and politics changed irrevocably in the age of Marius has a distinguished tradition in modern historiography. The Florentine writer and political thinker Niccolò Machiavelli (1469–1527), in his *Discourses on the First Decade of Livy* – a reflection on the foundations of power and the functioning of government, based on the model offered by the Roman Republic, written around 1517 and published posthumously in 1531 – established a strong link between the rise of Marius and the 'ruin' of the Republic (1.5), and argued that Marius was able to find soldiers that were prepared to 'forget about the Senate' and recognize him as its chief, because he was allowed to be in charge of the same army for a several consecutive years (3.24). The same point was made two centuries later by Charles de Montesquieu (1689–1755), a French political philosopher who wrote a formidably ambitious and highly influential essay on the causes of the success and downfall of ancient Rome (*Considerations on the Causes of the Greatness of the Romans and their Decline*, 1734). In his view, the expansion of the empire led to a gradual loosening of the ties between soldiers and Rome: within a few generations, there were no longer soldiers of the Republic, but soldiers of Marius or Sulla (Chapter 9).

The terms of the historiographical debate on this period have changed beyond recognition since Montesquieu's day, but the point that he made on Marius remains in a fundamental respect: his age was a period in which the very notion of what being Roman was about was profoundly redefined, and in which developments of major significance in the process that led to the end of the Roman Republic unfolded. The brief of this book is to discuss the role that Marius played in that process of change. The first step in this study must be a discussion of his background and his early years.

Marius' background

Gaius Marius was born in 158 or 157 BC at Arpinum, a town in Latium, about sixty miles south-east of Rome, in the valley of the river Liris (Liri), which had taken shape around a hilltop settlement. The exact date of birth is not attested, but may be reconstructed with some confidence on the basis of the stages of his later career and on the partly contradictory statements of some literary sources. The early inhabitants of Marius' hometown had been the Volsci, an Italian people that had migrated to southern Latium from the Apennines and spoke an Indo-European language that was fairly close to Latin and Umbrian. They were staunchly opposed to the Romans in the early Republican period, especially for the best part of the fifth century BC. That phase of conflict had, however, been followed by the gradual inclusion of the inhabitants of the region within the Roman dominions from the early fourth century BC and, in due course, into the Roman citizen body. Arpinum had been a community of Roman citizens since 188 BC, after having enjoyed a favourable legal status *vis-à-vis* Rome (the *ciuitas sine suffragio*, 'citizenship without voting rights') for more than a century. Latin was the language that the overwhelming majority of the inhabitants spoke and in which official business was conducted. Marius was part of the second generation of Roman citizens in his hometown: a community that, while being integrated with Rome, remained a free-standing, self-governing entity (*municipium*), with its own set of institutions and magistracies. For most of its citizens, as we shall see, the obvious way of seeking and obtaining prominence was to seek public office locally. Marius took an altogether different route, and an anything but obvious one.

The Greek writer Plutarch of Chaeronea (c. AD 46–120) opens his biography of Marius by establishing a very strong link between his origins and his politics. In his account, Marius was an outsider, and proudly so: he did not even grow up at Arpinum proper, but in the village of Cirrhaeton, which was part of the city's rural hinterland. Marius' legacy was so enduring in those parts that the inhabitants of that village would still call themselves *Mariani* in the first century AD, and a district in the modern township of Arpino still proudly bears the name 'Casamari' and is regarded locally as the place where Marius spent his early years. Plutarch points out that such a distinctively rural background sheltered Marius from the more sophisticated ways of the city and enabled him (paradoxically enough) to be raised in the values of traditional Roman virtue. Whether this was truly the case, it is impossible to establish. The ideological agenda of later sources plays an important part in sketching the portrait of a good true Roman who is committed to the good old ways of the ancestors. More generally, it would be unwise to draw any conclusions on Marius' character and personal beliefs from a body of evidence that is so heavily shaped by political bias and literary concerns, and is mostly derivative. The caveat does not apply just to Plutarch's work.

The biographer depicts Marius as someone who staunchly refused to learn Greek or to engage with all that Greek literature and thought had to offer; later in life he also refrained from using Greek in any matter of importance, including – we must assume – dealings with Greek-speaking political counterparts. In choosing that line of emphatic rejection Marius was retracing, no doubt intentionally, the footsteps of another great Italian outsider who reached considerable political prominence at Rome: M. Porcius Cato the Censor (234–149/148 BC), from Tusculum, a major figure in the first half of the second century BC. Cato is said to have pursued the study of Greek literature only in his old age, although what survives of his literary works shows a clear awareness of and familiarity with Greek literature that is at odds with that anecdote and with what we know of his public views on the value of Hellenic culture. The active role that Marius took later in life in dealing with the affairs of the Greek East suggests that a similar degree of doublespeak might have gone on in his case too.

Another feature of the ancient tradition on Marius' early years is equally puzzling, and indeed problematic. Marius' parents are said to have been of very modest social status: his father and namesake sustained his family, according to Plutarch, through manual labour, and Valerius Maximus (early first century AD), the author of a large collection of exemplary anecdotes, argues that Marius' inconspicuous social background was the factor that prevented him from embarking on a career in his home town. However, other pieces of evidence suggest a different account. Marius' sister is known to have married a man called M. Gratidius, who belonged to one of the most prominent families in Arpinum, and was in turn connected to the Tullii, another local family, to which the great orator M. Tullius Cicero (106–43 BC) belonged (see Marius' family tree, page 13). It is worth contemplating the possibility that Marius' family was in fact not of lowly status. It is at the same time easy to see why some ancient authors might have accepted the tradition on Marius' poverty and indeed found it attractive. On the one hand, it conveys the measure of Marius' achievement; on the other, it gives further depth to the image of Marius as a man wholly alien from the established elite, whether at Arpinum or at Rome, and bound to have some sympathy for the excluded and underprivileged, be they property-less soldiers or disenfranchised Italians. Things, as we shall see, were more complex than that.

Marius' family background may be elusive, but is instructive in another important respect: the name with which it endowed him. As Plutarch – a Greek intellectual who had a solid knowledge and understanding of things Roman – did not fail to notice, Marius did not have the three names that Roman citizens typically had in Plutarch's day (*praenomen, nomen,* and *cognomen*: e.g. Gaius Julius Caesar). In fact, by the late second century BC the three names were not as widespread as Plutarch suggests, even within the elite. However, Marius' name was a clear pointer to his Italian origins. Only one other Marius is attested in Rome before the late second century BC (Q. Marius, a junior magistrate who was involved in the running of the mint), while several Marii are recorded in inscriptions from southern Italy in this period. Moreover, 'Marius' was not just a gentilician name, but was also widely used as a personal name across central and southern Italy. It had a close parallel in the Oscan name *Maras*.

Like many young men of Italian background, Marius embarked on military service from a relatively early age. Again, the details are elusive. Plutarch places him in Spain during the early 130s, in the campaign against the Celtiberians that culminated with the siege and conquest of Numantia. During the final phase of the war he served under P. Cornelius Scipio Aemilianus (185–129 BC), the son of L. Aemilius Paullus Macedonicus, the victor of Pydna, and the adoptive grandson of Scipio Africanus. Aemilianus was arguably the

greatest military talent of his time: he had carried out the destruction
of Carthage in 146 BC, at the end of the Third Punic War. Unlike
Marius, he came from a family of great distinction, but Plutarch (and
his source) points out that the two men had some important common
ground: Aemilianus was very keen to restore high standards of discipline within the Roman ranks at a crucial junction of the campaign,
and he did not fail to see that Marius' ability and commitment enabled
him to stand out among his peers. The young man from Arpinum
received some formal recognition for his value, and even enjoyed the
privilege of dining with the commander. On one occasion, when he
flatteringly asked Aemilianus whether any future Roman commander
would ever be able to match his valour, he received an intriguing
reply: 'Maybe you will'. This is a very suspicious anecdote, but a
thought-provoking one for at least two reasons. On the one hand, it
belongs to a historical tradition that discusses the ability of Roman
great men to foresee and predict the future, the most notable instance
of which is Sulla's alleged prediction that allowing Caesar to survive
at the end of the Civil War would soon pose a fatal threat to the
Republic. On the other hand, it is a stark, perhaps extreme reminder
of what a powerful means of social and political rise military service
could be. The views on the importance of discipline and traditional
values that two men from very different backgrounds like Aemilianus
and Marius apparently shared belong in this very picture.

Recognizing that his military prowess played a major role in
Marius' rise does not amount to dismissing his social background
and overlooking that he had a recognizable political profile as early
as in his twenties. The problem is that the information on Marius'
early career is very fragmentary, and no coherent narrative may be
constructed without a considerable degree of speculation. This is
far from unusual in the history of the Roman Republic: educated
guesswork is often the best course of action, at least on matters
biographical. There is evidence that he held the office of military

tribune, a middle-ranking position in the army, for which twenty-four holders were elected by the people every year. Establishing a date is problematic: according to Sallust, when Marius stood for the military tribunate, he was not widely known among voters, but his deeds were, and that enabled him to obtain the support of the *comitia tributa*. How the news of Marius' achievements made it to Rome and circulated among the Roman populace is at best a matter for speculation – at any rate, that the fine military record of a young man would become a matter of wider interest is a feature of the Roman political debate, and it is noteworthy that this could steer the choices of the voters. We do not know what he did with the office to which he was elected. Rome's complex involvement across the Mediterranean did not fail to provide suitable opportunities: for example, it is conceivable (if by no means proven) that Marius might have served in the war that Rome fought in Asia Minor against Aristonicus (133–129), who claimed to be the half-brother of the late King Attalus III and opposed the annexation of the kingdom to the dominions of Rome, as provided in Attalus' will. The later development of Marius' career would prove the increasing significance of that region within the wider setup of the empire.

The context

In fact, the importance of Asia Minor within the wider context of Rome's Mediterranean hegemony had emphatically emerged in the weeks following Attalus III's decision to bequeath his kingdom to Rome, in 133 BC. The tribune Tiberius Sempronius Gracchus proposed to use the revenues generated by the new dominion in Western Asia Minor to fund the agrarian reform that he had just passed and to purchase more public land for distribution to the poor throughout Italy. His plan envisaged a method of exploiting the rewards of the Empire for which there was no precedent, and was quickly rebuffed. It was probably a decisive factor in prompting the decision of a section of the senatorial nobility to launch a violent attack on Tiberius and his supporters, in which the tribune lost his life. A decade later, his brother Gaius held the same office and put forward a proposal for the organization of tax collection across the province of Asia. The task was entrusted to private companies, owned and run by members of the equestrian order, on the basis of public auctions that were to be held every five years. It was as sophisticated a system of extracting resources from the province as it was ruthless: the tax collectors, known as *publicani*, were at liberty to make as large a profit as they wished. The predictable outcome was decades of ruthless exploitation of the province, and a legacy of deep resentment towards Rome in that region, which would not fail to unleash heavy consequences in a few decades' time.

Gaius Gracchus was mindful of the need to secure an effective exploitation of the empire, and was also keen to attract support from the equestrian order. He knew that his brother Tiberius had managed to attract the support of large sectors of the rural plebs to his agrarian reform, but was otherwise rather isolated in Rome. Even large sectors of the urban populace sided with his enemies. Gaius intended to revive the project of land reform and embark on other initiatives of comparable ambition; he therefore worked to create as broad a coalition as conceivably possible. That strategy enabled him to secure the passing of a number of significant measures, including a law that set up subsidized corn distributions to the people of Rome, and to secure election to the tribunate for two years in a row. It also did not fail to attract considerable opposition from sectors of the senatorial elite, which started to work for the repeal of Gracchus' legislation. The assassination of the attendant of L. Opimius, one of the consuls of 121, by some supporters of Gracchus gave the Senate grounds for passing an emergency decree (a *senatus consultum ultimum*) that instructed the consuls to take whatever action might be needed to restore order and avert the threat to the stability of the state. Gaius Gracchus and a large number of his supporters lost their lives in the ensuing riot: unlike Tiberius and his associates in 133, they were eliminated in an action that had the formal endorsement of the Senate, and for which a much clearer legal case could be made.

We do not know what Marius' stance in that period was, although the evidence for his later connection with the Metelli suggests that he probably did not find himself among Gracchus' supporters; a decade earlier, he had been serving in Spain while Tiberius Gracchus was polarizing opinions in Rome. However, when the Gracchan crisis unfolded, Marius was a young man who was just beginning to consider his options. Whatever his role and allegiance might have been in those years, the events must have deeply shaped his perception and understanding of politics.

The Gracchan crisis was not just about land reform and the balance of power between Senate and people. It was also a moment in which violence was deployed on a large scale to solve a political crisis and also early emergence of a pattern that developed much further during Marius' lifetime. Montesquieu might have regarded the age of Marius as a turning point in Roman history. A number of ancient writers, however, placed the watershed in the decline of the Republic with the age of the Gracchi. Both periodizations are legitimate, and draw attention to different aspects of the crisis: the emergence of major political and social questions in 133, and the relationship between politics and warfare in the age of Marius and Sulla.

Other ancient accounts of the late Republican period put forward a different view of the moment in which things started to unravel in Rome. Most notably, Sallust identified the fall and destruction of Carthage in 146 BC as *the* turning point. The obliteration of Rome's fiercest enemy brought home a point that had already been clear since the victory against Hannibal, half a century earlier: Rome was the dominant power in the Mediterranean world, and no viable alternative to her hegemony existed. After 146, there was not even the remote prospect of Carthage reviving its long-lost power. In fact, the rationale followed by many advocates of the attack against the city, most notably Cato the Elder, was that the potential threat of a Carthaginian comeback had to be pre-empted. In Sallust's view, the unrivalled supremacy that Rome had achieved turned into a source of moral disorder and political disruption. The lack of an external threat made people complacent, and readily persuaded the political elite that there was no longer a compelling need to secure concord and orderly cooperation within the community. Unrestrained political competition and shameless display of wealth ensued. The political crisis of the late Republic was rooted, according to that narrative, in a set of moral developments. No modern student of this period would subscribe to that account, but the view that there was a link between the expansion of the empire and the traumatic political developments of the last century of the Republic retains great explanatory power. It is also central to the understanding of Marius' agenda.

The family of Gaius Marius

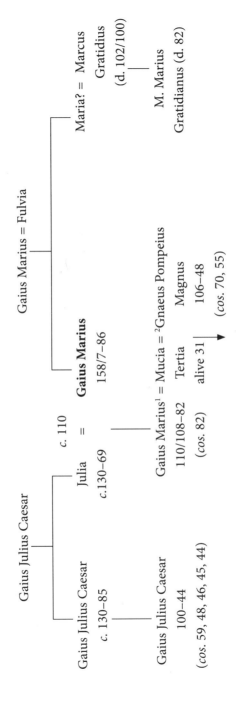

2

Marius' Rise

Marius' early career

We can find a full list of the public offices held by Marius in an inscription in his honour that was on display in the Forum of Augustus at Rome, and was part of a larger cycle of dedications honouring a number of distinguished Romans. The original does not survive, but a full copy of the text on display at Rome was found at Arretium (modern Arezzo) in Etruria. Like most celebratory inscriptions of this kind (known as *elogia*), it conveys a neatly linear account of the honorand's career. Some evidence, however, puts that picture into question. Valerius Maximus singled out Marius as a prime example in his discussion of the mutations of Fortune and the relationship that these have with the development of one's character. In doing so, he developed a tradition that, as we shall see in the final chapter of this book, had been sympathetically developed by Marius' fellow-citizen and long-time admirer Cicero: Marius was a model of resilience and resolve before the fickleness and treacherousness of fate (and, indeed, of many of his contemporaries). The whole of Marius' rise to prominence was, in Valerius Maximus' view, a contest against unfavourable factors. First he stood for office at Arpinum, his hometown, and was not judged of sufficient standing for that. After that electoral defeat, he stood for the quaestorship (a junior magistracy that involved financial or administrative duties) in Rome. Valerius suggests that his first attempt was unsuccessful: he speaks of 'rebuffs' (*repulsae*), which, however, did not prevent him from obtaining the quaestorship and joining the senatorial order. His rise to the more senior magistracies was not any easier. He just managed to get elected to the aedileship and the praetorship (two magistracies that pertained to the upkeep of the city of Rome and to the administration of justice respectively). In the latter case he was at the bottom of the list of the successful candidates. Such an undistinguished start would have made the following development of Marius' career very surprising: no one could have predicted that the man from Arpinum who struggled his way up through the ranks would manage to get elected to the consulship, and would eventually hold the senior office of the Republic seven times.

It is easy to see how this account makes a very fascinating story, and one that is of immediate relevance to an author like Valerius, who is keen to provide his audience with neat, memorable moral examples. Valerius was very well read, and it is likely that some of the information that he provides in his discussion of this issue is factually correct. But there are at least two important provisos to make. He makes no mention of Marius' military tribunate, and of the service that the reputation he had earned on campaign made to his career; and he does not acknowledge a well-known fact in Republican politics. Aediles were typically expected to make part of their personal assets available for the organization of the public games for which they had responsibility. This seems to be very much at odds with the lowly (*humilis*) social status that Marius allegedly had, not just in Rome, but in Arpinum too. Although hardly anything is known about Marius' family background, the trajectory of his career strongly suggests that he did not just have a conspicuous military talent to offer to the Republic, but that he could also rely on reasonably strong financial assets. Like many members of the municipal elites who tried the path of public office in Rome, he could make use of those resources in an increasingly tight political competition.

Money was not enough to secure election to public office, especially if one were to set one's eyes on the more prestigious magistracies. Marius' military skills certainly worked in his favour and earned him a reasonable degree of notoriety; but connections with sectors of the political elite were at least as valuable. The support of men that had already held senior public offices and belonged to families that had already produced consuls in the past could have both direct and indirect advantages. It enabled an ambitious candidate to rely on the electoral support of the voters that had bonds of loyalty and patronage with those families, and gave them clout and authoritativeness before the wider political community. Plutarch claims that the beginning of the political career of Marius, after his distinguished service at Numantia, was made possible by his personal connection with 'Caecilius Metellus', who played a major role in securing his election to the tribunate of the plebs. The identity of this individual is not certain, but his political and social profile is very clear: the Caecilii Metelli were a family of great distinction, from which a remarkable sequence of consuls had hailed in the previous generations. Marius' supporter is probably to be chosen between Q. Caecilius Metellus Baliaricus (*cos.* 123) and L. Caecilius Metellus Delmaticus (*cos.* 119). The names of both men point to their military record: respectively, to a victory against a fleet of pirates near the Balearic Islands, in 122, and to one in Dalmatia, on the eastern coast of the Adriatic, in 117. The social gulf between the Metelli and a man of Marius' background was considerable, and must have been obvious to all their contemporaries. Plutarch notes that the connection with Marius extended to the previous generations: Metellus had been a patron of the Marii of Arpinum. It was not uncommon for influential families of Rome to have connections with distinguished families of the cities of Italy, whether they were from communities of Roman citizens, like Arpinum, or not. If Plutarch's account were accurate, the tradition of Marius' lowly origins would be conclusively undermined.

The biographer explains Marius' first electoral success with the close ties that he had with a family that had a central place in the Roman political elite and a very significant position within the senatorial order. That is a striking twist in the career of a man who built much of his credentials as an outsider. The paradox is further emphasized by the fact that the support of the Metelli enabled him to get elected to the tribunate of the plebs, the magistracy that was traditionally entrusted with the protection of the interests of the members of the Roman plebs against the abuses of the magistrates and the patricians. In the previous decades, as we have seen, the tribunate had increasingly become an outlet of instances of political and social reform: most importantly, the cause of the agrarian reform and of a fairer distribution of public land, which the Gracchi had advocated between the 130s and the 120s, raising intense controversy. However, it would be misguided to regard the tribunate as a constant force of political reform. Its role in the Republic was much more complex and problematic. This is chiefly because, like all the Roman magistracies, it was a collegial one: ten tribunes were elected every year, and they all had the power to block the initiatives of one of their colleagues, as well as those of the other magistrates (often referred to in English as 'veto power': *veto* is the Latin for 'I forbid'). The college of the tribunes, therefore, could realistically work only if there was broad consensus on a policy advocated by the tribunes, and it was fairly easy for the opponents of reforms, and for the most influential sectors of the senatorial nobility, to have some of their favourite candidates elected.

Even if we were to accept Plutarch's account that Marius owed his election to the tribunate to the patronage of the Metelli, his work as a tribune was not just led by the wish to please the senatorial nobility. On the contrary, he was the initiator of a significant reform: a law that narrowed the bridges on which voters were expected to walk to the spot where they were supposed to cast their ballots. Cicero, who approvingly acknowledged the importance of this law more than half a century after its passing, argued that its chief aim was to prevent electoral corruption; restricting the passages also had the effect of reducing the possibility of intimidation or harassment. On the face of it, therefore, the law passed by Marius was informed by the need to secure fairer elections, in which the will of the people could emerge more freely. Moreover, it was not an isolated measure, but belonged in a context that had recently witnessed important changes in the ways in which the voting assemblies of the Roman people functioned: in 139 a law proposed by the tribune A. Gabinius introduced the secret ballot in elections, and in 137 a law put forward by the tribune L. Cassius Longinus Ravilla extended to the cases in which the people were summoned to vote as a jury in a trial (except for cases of *perduellio*, roughly equating to high treason).

There is little doubt that in some quarters these were seen as major shifts in the way in which politics worked in Rome: the new ways in which voting operations took place are depicted on a coin issued in this period, probably in 113 BC (*Roman Republican Coinage* 292/1), in which two voters are depicted on the passageway where the voting operation is meant to be take place; the one on the left receives the ballot from an attendant below, and another one on the right casts his ballot in an urn. The scene is ostensibly depicted because of its political implications, and the significance that the reform had: it may be directly connected to the law passed during Marius' tribunate. Plutarch also understood the reform put forward by Marius as a political innovation that upset the hegemony of the Senate, opposed by the consul L. Aurelius Cotta; Marius was reportedly summoned before the Senate to defend his conduct, but proudly defended his policy. Not even Metellus' open opposition persuaded him to revisit his attitude: on the contrary, he used the full extent of his powers of tribune of the plebs and ordered his ally to be arrested. Remarkably, none of the other tribunes found the courage to veto Marius' initiative; the Senate had no choice but to withdraw its opposition and the bill was duly passed.

Plutarch is notoriously keen to depict the politics of the late Republican period as the story of the opposition between Senate and people, and it is quite likely that features of this story were exaggerated, especially in light of Marius' later achievements. Emphasizing the extent of his rift with Metellus, for example, serves well the purposes of an account of the life of a man who had an extraordinarily eventful and complex career, as Valerius Maximus also pointed out. In fact, the development of Marius' relationship with the Metelli at this crucial junction does not receive a satisfactory account in any of the surviving sources. We may well be facing an anachronism shaped by the later developments in Marius' career. But there is no reason to disbelieve Valerius' account in one important respect: Marius had an original and complex political agenda. Arguably, he was able and willing to think about politics along more creative and ambitious lines than those of many of his opponents. Many of his long-term and shorter-term objectives, however, remain elusive. We can only speculate, for example, on the reasons that led him to oppose a bill that provided for corn distributions to the Roman people, probably expanding the scope of a law passed by the tribune Gaius Gracchus in 122 BC, which had introduced heavily subsidized handouts. The principle that the poor could be entitled to food handouts was heavily contested by members of the senatorial nobility, and such opposition was one of the main arguments invoked by the movement that rallied against Gracchus. Surely in opposing the corn bill Marius pursued two aims, not necessarily incompatible with one another: on the one hand, he might have intended to stress that he was not following in the mould of the Gracchi and to avoid a violent reaction against him; on the other, he might have sought an opportunity to mend fences with the Metelli and their supporters within the Senate.

His ambition was certainly that of continuing along the path of what the Romans called the *cursus honorum*, the 'path of the public offices': the obvious step forward, after the tribunate of the plebs, was the aedileship, a magistracy that entailed a complex set of responsibilities, both in the public and in the religious domains. As we have seen, holding that office required a very solid financial position: the aediles were expected to make some of their own resources available for the organization of public games. While his decision to stand for the aedileship is a clear indication of Marius' good economic position and further undermines the hypothesis that he had a lowly background, success was not a foregone conclusion in such a competitive field. Indeed, according to Cicero, Marius was defeated in two elections; Plutarch recounts a partly different story, whereby Marius first stood for election to the curule aedileship and later decided to stand for election to the less prestigious class of aediles (the plebeian one), when he realized that he had no chance of being elected to the curule rank. This belated, almost clumsy political move did not spare him defeat; he therefore failed to be elected twice in the same year (probably 116).

That remarkable failure did not mark the end of Marius' political ambitions. Both Valerius Maximus and Plutarch speak of his election to the praetorship, the next higher office in the ranking of public offices, and stress that Marius' election was very narrow: he came at the bottom of the list of the successful candidates. Moreover, doubts were soon cast on the grounds of his success: he was prosecuted on electoral corruption charges. Such an allegation was not uncommon in Republican Rome: criminal cases were not initiated by the government – Rome had nothing resembling a Crown Prosecution Service – but were brought by individuals who had access to relevant information. Even when they were substantial, therefore, they were likely to be politically motivated. The case against Marius was no exception, and the Metelli were almost certainly among its backers, if not among its initiators. Ironically, the recent changes to the voting procedure that he had contributed to bringing about played an important role in the prosecution's case. A slave of Cassius Sabaco, a close friend of Marius, was found in the sector where the voting was due to take place; his presence was regarded as a direct indication that he was intending to influence the electoral process. Sabaco pointed out that his slave only intended to bring him water as the voting was taking place, and that the incident was therefore entirely innocent. Evidence was also sought from others, including a man called C. Herennius, who claimed that he could not give evidence against Marius because he was a long-time client of his; interestingly, Marius took issue with this claim and argued that the magistracy that he had held set him free from any previous bond of *clientela*. The point was dubious, but the anecdote is further testimony to Marius' increasing social and positive standing. The trial had a positive outcome for Marius, albeit by a narrow margin: the jury, which was made up of members of the equestrian order – the same social group from which Marius hailed – could not reach a clear verdict and Marius was acquitted.

He could therefore take up the praetorship, a prestigious public office that opened up valuable avenues of political and institutional activity for him, whether in overseeing the hearing of criminal or civil cases, or in aspects of the administration of the city of Rome. Unfortunately, no information survives on Marius' work during his magistracy. The official activity of the praetors, however, was not confined to the tenure of their magistracy. Once they left office they were typically deployed in the provinces that Rome controlled across the empire, usually in charge of a contingent of troops, and often entrusted with the running of military operations. It is quite possible that the prospect of Marius' holding a military command in the not too distant future played a part in influencing the choice of the voters. At any rate, when he relinquished office he was dispatched to the province of Further Spain (*Hispania Ulterior*), in the south-west of the Iberian peninsula, a region that had been under the jurisdiction of Roman governors since the early second century. The province was in an unstable situation, apparently because of the presence of gangs of robbers that threatened the very functioning of government. Marius took them on and succeeded in restraining their action. His victory is likely to have received some recognition, although he was not granted a triumph, the highest military honour to which a victorious general could aspire.

Plutarch notes that the provincial governorship did not enable Marius to become wealthy, as was often the case with many Roman magistrates at the end of their tenure overseas: extracting as much revenue from a province as conceivably possible was a straightforward (if morally objectionable and at times politically unwise) device for former magistrates to recover from the major expenditure that they had incurred during their election campaign. Marius apparently followed a different model of behaviour, in keeping with the commitment to traditional values and virtues that the ancient sources credit him with. He used his governorship to forge valuable political ties within the province, especially among the many Roman citizens who resided there and were involved in business activities, while retaining connections in their Italian hometowns: those would prove useful in the years to come, and not just for electoral purposes. More significantly, his governorship did not provide his enemies with any grounds for another prosecution. Marius could look forward to planning his bid for the consulship, which was the obvious career step for a former praetor (although the law prescribed a gap of at least three years between the two magistracies, preparing a campaign was no mean feat). He was, by that point, a respected and well-known member of the Senate – not a stellar candidate, to be sure, but a political player that could not be lightly dismissed.

Like any serious political player, he had influential supporters and committed enemies. His friend Sabaco was expelled from the Senate in the year following the imbroglio that had preceded the prosecution of Marius. The decision fell within the remit of the censors, two senior magistrates who had, among their duties, the official review of the senatorial order. Sabaco's conduct before and during the trial was deemed unworthy of a senator, and that was a typical reason that was given for deciding the expulsion of a member. The decision, however, was not merely a procedural one, and always entailed a political judgement on the censors' part. Sanctioning a close friend of Marius was also an attack on Marius himself. The senior statesmen that served as censors in the year 115 BC were Cn. Domitius Ahenobarbus and L. Caecilius Metellus Delmaticus: it is unsurprising to find a Metellus taking a measure that was to affect Marius' position.

However, that setback did not seriously undermine his prospects. It is probably in the period following his governorship in Spain that we can place his marriage to Iulia, a member of the patrician family of the Iulii Caesares. That was a remarkable achievement for a man who could not claim a single member of the senatorial order in his family history. The Iulii Caesares were not among the most influential families in Roman politics, but had a distinguished background, and even numbered among those families that traced their history back to the origins of Rome, and claimed direct descent from the goddess Venus and her son, the Trojan prince Aeneas. Scholars have often found it hard to escape the temptation of explaining marriages within the Roman elite with narrow political or economic explanations. The marriage of Marius and Iulia does not necessarily imply that the Iulii Caesares were unanimously backing Marius and his likely bid for the consulship, nor should it be seen as evidence that they were prepared to renounce their aristocratic credentials in exchange for a connection with a capable and ambitious young man. Although marriages could and often did have political implications, the union of Marius and Iulia should not be read in a narrow political sense, or as part of his imminent attempt to stand for the consulship. It was, however, a symptom of the credibility that Marius had gained among important sectors of the traditional Roman elite.

The Jugurthine War

The rise of Marius to the consulship was eventually determined by a major shift in the political climate, which intervened quite suddenly, although it did have deep roots in the way in which Roman foreign policy had been conducted over the previous decades. Its background was a situation of instability far away from Rome, in the kingdom of Numidia, in North Africa. The local dynast Jugurtha had recently usurped the throne by assassinating his adoptive brothers Hiempsal and Adherbal, after their father Micipsa had entrusted the rule of the kingdom to the three of them upon his death in 118. Rome had been a long-time ally of the kingdom of Numidia and of its immediate neighbour, Mauretania; the province of Africa, which included the region surrounding Carthage, was also an immediate neighbour of Numidia. It was unsurprising that Rome would take an interest in the crisis, and it was quite typical of its conduct in this period to get actively involved in the problems that affected its allies with a view to bringing about a solution that would not harm its interests. There was at first some hesitation about embarking on a military campaign. Action became inevitable after Jugurtha attacked Adherbal at Cirta and a number of Italian businessmen were killed as they were taking part in the defence. L. Calpurnius Bestia (*cos.* 111) failed to make any progress in the campaign and offered Jugurtha a peace deal. It was widely alleged that the bribes that Jugurtha paid to him and various leading figures within the Senate played a crucial role in determining that outcome. Jugurtha was summoned to Rome to give evidence in the case against Bestia, but was forbidden to do so by the intervention of a tribune, and therefore returned to Africa. The Roman campaign continued under the ineffective leadership of Sp. Postumius Albinus (*cos.* 110), and later under the considerably more capable Q. Caecilius Metellus (*cos.* 109), who was in charge of operations for two years.

This conflict is not a moment of major importance in the history of Roman imperialism, but is an event about which we are relatively well informed, because it attracted the interest of Sallust, who wrote a full account of the war nearly eighty years after the event, in an historical work entitled *The Jugurthine War* (*Bellum Jugurthinum*). His interest was not so much in the military aspects of the conflict nor in the history of the Roman conquest of North Africa, although he did offer plenty of insights on those issues. On the contrary, he was deeply interested in what the war against Jugurtha and the events surrounding it could reveal about the decline and fall of the Roman Republic (a process that had come to a tragic end during his own lifetime). The dealings between the Senate and the Numidian king denounced, in his view, the incompetence of the political elite and the ease with which it could be bribed into inaction by a ruthless operator. More generally, corruption is rooted in the flux of unprecedented volumes of wealth from overseas to Rome and the increasing competition for public office that it prompted in Rome. As Sallust memorably put it, in the city that was the mistress of the world, everything turned out to be up for sale. The Senate lacked a clear strategy on Numidia as it did on most other issues, and appeared to be driven only by the ambition to perpetuate its position of influence and privilege at the expense of the people, who were sidelined from key political decisions. The war against Jugurtha, however, was the moment in which that dysfunctional model faced a major crisis and showed all its inadequacies. The involvement in the operations of Marius and Sulla was not just the factor that paved the way for Rome's success, but a symptom that new forces were shaping up on the horizon and were getting ready for changing the political game for good. They also forebode a political season in which the role of some prominent individuals (not necessarily hailing from the most distinguished families in the city) was to become central. Sallust played a distinctive role in sketching the image of Marius as a pivotal figure in the late Republican period, one that is associated with the onset of a period of major historical change.

Sallust was not an uncritical admirer of Marius, nor indeed of Sulla. He does not make any attempt to conceal that his rise to the consulship was somewhat indebted to the use of ruthless methods. We are suddenly presented with a rather different portrait from that of the overachieving outsider committed to military discipline, and come to see a less edifying image of a former praetor who is prepared to make every conceivable effort to attain the consulship. In 109 BC, after two years of largely fruitless campaigning, the consul Q. Caecilius Metellus took the helm of the operations. Sallust depicts him as a man who did not share the flaws of many of his peers and contemporaries, but points out that his army lacked the discipline and rigour to live up to his example. There may well be an element of literary or moralistic exaggeration in this remark. At any rate, the campaign was a complex military operation, which required a sustained military strategy. From the early stages of the mission Marius served on Metellus' staff as a *legatus*, a senior aide de camp, apparently with special responsibility for the cavalry: a task that required a reasonably solid working relationship with the consul. The evidence for the connection between Marius and the Metelli in the preceding years would appear to make that scenario unlikely. While the task of *legatus* would certainly have been appealing to Marius, who no doubt intended to boost his credentials as a prospective candidate for the consulship, it is less apparent why Metellus would have wished to offer Marius this opportunity to display his calibre. It cannot be ruled out that Marius had mended fences with the Metelli in the previous few years. It is also equally possible that Metellus just decided to associate himself with one of the best military talents of his time. Marius certainly had the ability to make a remarkable contribution in several respects. Plutarch notes that through his willingness to share the toils and labours of the soldiers he fostered a sense of camaraderie and cohesion within the ranks that served the cause of the campaign, while at the same time serving his reputation in Rome. Sallust also records his contribution to some operations early on in the war, such as the conquest of the town of Sicca, which had been the first community to defect from Jugurtha, and the inconclusive siege of Zama, which he conducted together with Metellus.

There is no evidence for outstanding feats on Marius' part during the campaign, but his record appears to have been sufficiently solid to enable him to nurture his ambitions and to cause tensions with Metellus. The incident involving T. Turpilius Silanus, a close friend of Metellus, was a source of further controversy and a symptom of Marius' increasing (and, from Metellus' viewpoint, unwelcome) independence. Turpilius, then *praefectus fabrum* (a title that may loosely be translated as 'chief of staff') of Metellus, was in charge of a Roman garrison in the town of Vaga. Jugurtha managed to get into the city thanks to the support of the inhabitants; Turpilius was released unharmed, but the incident prompted a prosecution on charges of treason before Metellus and his advisory council. According to Plutarch, Marius argued for the death penalty, which Metellus was forced to accept. When, sometime later, the charge was proved to be false, Marius claimed that the conviction had been instigated by Metellus. Sallust makes no reference to this incident, but also agrees that the differing agendas of the two men had made that disagreement inevitable.

It is a safe guess that the Turpilius affair diminished Metellus' standing. The differences between the two ancient accounts, however, are an indication of the existence of conflicting traditions on that episode. This is, as we shall see, not an unparalleled feature in the evidence for Marius' life and career. The events in Numidia were

deeply divisive, and the assessment of them impinged on the circumstances that led to Marius' rise to power as much as on his character.
An important point should not be overlooked. Both Plutarch and
Sallust pursue complex literary agendas, and are keen to use these
events as opportunities to construct and give further depth to the
main characters in the plot they are telling. These choices also affect
the way in which the narrative is constructed: Plutarch dates the affair
of Turpilius before the rift between Marius and Metellus and singles
it out as a major factor for it, while Sallust places it at a later time.
Whatever solution may be preferable, this is a sobering instance of
the limits of the ancient evidence and of the caution with which it
should be approached. A coherent account of a set of events is not
necessarily a factually accurate one.

The same proviso should apply to the events that led to Marius'
decision to put forward his candidacy to the consulship. In Plutarch's
account Marius entertains the ambition of standing for the highest
office throughout the campaign, and is eager to be dismissed by
Metellus and be allowed to go to Rome to present his candidacy.
Metellus agreed to let him leave only twelve days before the elections
were due to take place (the date is not on record), with a deliberate
intention to damage his chances, and Marius had to travel from
the camp to the city of Utica, from where he would take a ship to
Rome. Just before setting off he performed a sacrifice, during which
a haruspex – one of the Etruscan diviners that routinely assisted
Roman magistrates in the performance of their duties – foretold
unprecedented success for him. In Sallust's narrative the prophecy is
the event that persuades Marius to overcome any hesitation and put
forward his name: until then, he is a loyal, or at least cooperative,
associate of Metellus, and is reluctant to seek the consulship because
of his undistinguished origins and his status of 'new man'. This is not
just a turning point in Marius' career, but in his character: until then
he had held all his offices with a skill and a dedication that were more

commensurate with higher offices; afterwards he was driven by an ambition that no longer had any restraint. Sallust is deeply interested in decline and degeneration, and in the turning points that mark such developments. It is significant that the prophecy of a foreign religious expert – another outsider – plays a central part in Marius' choices and in shaping his later fortune. In Sallust's account, Metellus attempts to persuade Marius not to pursue the consulship, mainly by using the typical argument of the senatorial elite, and which Marius himself had long accepted: the consulship is not a suitable brief for someone with a background like his. Metellus is depicted as a typical member of his social group: he has talent and prestige, but is driven by a deep-seated sense of the entitlement that his condition implies, and can be arrogant towards his counterparts. The result of his reaction was to spark resentment, and indeed, hatred towards him on Marius' part; in turn, it fuelled his ambition, and eventually clouded the judgement of one of the most capable men in Rome. In Sallust's vision, the negative consequences of the inability of the nobles to rise to the challenge of the present times are very far-reaching indeed.

Marius did little to downplay his rift with Metellus. Quite the contrary, he apparently based his own campaign for the consulship on a clear opposition between himself – the new man with impeccable military credentials, who promised to deal definitively with Jugurtha – and Metellus – the member of a corrupt and degenerate elite who had failed to make any progress against the king. Significantly, he had himself introduced to the popular gathering where he presented his candidature through the agency of a tribune. His work, however, had been carefully prepared well before his return: Sallust mentions the lobbying that Marius had been doing among the Roman traders based at Utica, whom he briefed against Metellus and who in turn wrote letters to their connections back home, inviting them to support Marius. A further indication in the change of mood among the Roman people may be found in the passing of the *lex Mamilia*, under which prosecutions were initiated against those who were accused of having taken bribes from Jugurtha, in 110 or 109. That contributed to improving his prospects; the reports coming from Africa did the rest. Sallust openly acknowledges that it was not the time for a cool evaluation of the merits of the candidates, and that many were driven by their passions, even more than by material considerations. The momentum was with Marius, and his election to the consulship was secured by a large consensus: the craftsmen in the city workshops and the peasants were his main supporters.

Marius' election was a remarkable event in another important respect: he was the first man without a senatorial background – a new man, a *homo novus* – to be elected to the most senior magistracy in a quarter of a century (P. Rupilius, *cos.* 132 BC, had been a tax collector in Sicily). While not an unprecedented development, it was certainly noteworthy. Sallust points out that the nobility was stunned by Marius' election. The surviving evidence does not record the names of his competitors, nor does it shed any details on how the election unfolded in practice. What appears with sufficient clarity is that the election to the consulship was merely the necessary step for the goal that Marius had kept in sight for some time: the return to Numidia and the launch of a new offensive against Jugurtha. To secure that aim, he had to undertake a political initiative that ran against the grain of established practice: he arranged for a tribune of the plebs, T. Manlius Mancinus, to ask the people who they wished to be in charge of the war. The assignment of a provincial command by the vote of the people was not just an act that, as far as we can tell, did not have any precedents in constitutional practice. It was, first and foremost, an open attack on the established authority of the Senate, which had already decreed the extension of the provincial command of Metellus. Sallust does not expand on the details of the process, and simply notes that the decision of the Senate was overridden by the will of the people.

The main task of a consul who was entrusted with the running of a military campaign was the recruitment of an army. Under the Republic, soldiers were not enlisted on a permanent, or even long-term capacity. Military levies took place on a regular basis, as Rome ran a number of campaigns, sometimes simultaneous: their handling was entrusted to the serving magistrates, who would have the responsibility for raising, training and leading their own army. The system was very well honed by the time Marius took up the consulship, although it was also being put under a complex set of pressures. There had been a number of episodes of resistance to military conscription throughout the second century, with the tribunes openly challenging the decisions of the consuls. In 151 BC they even advocated and eventually secured the arrest of the consuls A. Postumius Albinus and L. Licinius Lucullus for allegedly abusing their power in conducting the levy (an episode that reveals concerns and tensions over the issue of military recruitment). In the 130s and 120s the Gracchi argued that the unequal distribution of land across Italy did not just pose an issue of social justice, but was a fundamental threat to the stability of Rome and her ability to sustain the empire: a depopulated countryside and low agricultural productivity resulted in low birth rate and in a population decline that would in due course deprive the community of the manpower that was required to staff the army adequately. This is the picture that several ancient sources convey of the views and agendas of the Gracchi, and for a long time it was unproblematically accepted in modern scholarship. The archaeological work that was carried out in Italy in the second half of the twentieth century and some ground-breaking work on the demography of the peninsula in antiquity have gone a long way to invalidating this picture: there was no demonstrable crisis of small landholding in Italy, and there is no straightforward evidence for demographic decline in the Republican period. The debate on the demography of Roman Italy, in fact, remains open, and widely different views have been put forward over the last two decades. Still, it is likely that the Gracchi, many of their contemporaries in Rome, and most of the ancient authors that dealt with the problem were genuinely persuaded that there was a serious agrarian and demographic crisis, which had to be addressed by an ambitious political strategy. The ancient accounts of the recruitment methods that Marius used during his consulship must be read against this background.

Sallust stresses that Marius displayed his customary energy in the recruitment: he looked for reinforcements in Rome and across Italy, and personally sought to enlist the strongest men from the Italian cities and encouraged the discharged veterans to extend their service. He did not just rely on his office, his personal prestige, and his status of new man. He also drew the attention of his audience to the prospect of substantial war booty. He met with a warm reaction. The long speech that Sallust lends him in a remarkable passage of the *Jugurthine War* is almost certainly not a summary of a speech that Marius actually gave in the run-up to the war, but it is likely to be a plausible reflection of the arguments that he deployed: a rhetoric in which the merits of the commander and the duty to serve the Republic were at the forefront, but in which the tangible rewards of the campaign were unapologetically set out. That a consul would address his fellow-citizens during the preparation of the campaign was of course not unusual. We just happen to be relatively well informed about the events of 108 BC thanks to Sallust's decision to devote a whole historical monograph to the account of *that* war.

What is arguably more noteworthy is the process that Marius followed in carrying out the levy. According to Sallust, after having taken care of the supplies, he started to enrol soldiers chosen from the whole of the citizen body, without discriminating according to the census class to which they belonged, and including in the army all those who volunteered to serve – even if they did not have any property and belonged to the class that the Romans labelled *proletarii* ('proletarians' – literally: 'child-givers', i.e. people who can contribute to the commonwealth only through their offspring, *proles*). This practice was in clear discontinuity with the established practice of the ancestors: its immediate result was the recruitment of a considerably larger army than initially decided, and presumably agreed with the Senate. Sallust lucidly sets out the two different, although not necessarily incompatible explanations that were offered at the time for Marius' choice. Some argued that it was the response to a dearth of citizens with higher property qualifications. Others wryly pointed out that Marius coveted the favour of the poor, who had supported his rise to power and looked ahead at the prospect of war with nothing to lose and the eagerness to yield great material rewards. As we shall see, this line of explanation has found wide acceptance, well beyond antiquity. Plutarch also stresses that Marius' decision ran against the established practice, but suggests that the most controversial action of the new consul was his choice to denounce the abuses and vexations of the nobility, and especially of the members that had been involved in the campaign. The attention that he reserves to this aspect of Marius' conduct is a pointer to the actual extent and significance of the recruitment measure that he took.

However, the extent of the change introduced during the levy of 107 BC should not be overestimated. It belongs, in fact, within a longer-term development, which had led to the revision of the property qualification thresholds that were used in the recruitment operations. The census level that was expected of the members of the class of the *assidui*, the lowest class who were entitled to serve in the army, had gradually been decreasing, and the distinction between *assidui* (who could be enrolled) and *proletarii* (who were not eligible) had become minimal. Marius had a very urgent need to secure a speedy levy, and for that reason he introduced two changes that, while important, confirmed a trend that had already begun: volunteers could be drafted at very short notice, and widening the constituency of those who were eligible to serve would increase Marius' chance. *Proletarii* had been enlisted earlier at times of crisis, and the presence of volunteers in the army was usual. Moreover, the *proletarii* that Marius chose to enlist were not considerably poorer than many of the soldiers that were serving in his army. The levy of 107 was not the major reform that has often been envisaged, but a thoughtful and ambitious measure that reflects the ambition of Marius and his willingness to use innovative methods to achieve his aims and further his interests. Arguably, what is more significant from an historical standpoint and was more impressive to Marius' contemporaries is the kind of leadership that he displayed, and the bond that he succeeded in creating with his army. The strong motivation of the contingent of volunteers that he had recruited played an important part in that development.

His promise of material rewards was fulfilled shortly after the arrival of the army in Africa. The booty that was seized in the early stages of the operations was distributed among the troops; within a short time, new recruits and veterans alike were equally committed to the campaign. The overall strategy pursued by Marius, however, was not immune from difficulties: despite some small-scale success, there was no substantial breakthrough against Jugurtha in open field. Marius therefore decided to launch a series of sieges of the main cities that were loyal to the king. The siege of Capsa was the first major challenge that Marius had to face, despite a lack of corn supplies, which the Numidians had requisitioned from the surrounding countryside. The military confrontation that took place outside the city walls ended with the success of the Romans and the surrender of the inhabitants: that, however, was not sufficient to stop the Roman offensive and to prevent the destruction of the city and the massacre of the population. The inhabitants that were not killed were sold into slavery and – tellingly – the booty was distributed among Marius' soldiers. Even Sallust notes that Marius' conduct was against the code of war (*ius belli*) that any Roman commander was expected to adhere to. In the same breath, he also points out that the strategic advantage of that victory was considerable, as were the psychological consequences for the Numidians. Marius turned into a feared and widely respected enemy. The momentum of the campaign was suddenly with him: many came to regard his actions as divinely inspired, and not merely shaped by his own insight and courage. Sallust has little time for this sort of approach to the political dimension, and is all too keen to explore the limits and deficiencies in Marius' leadership. His account of the siege of the fortress of Capsa is revealing: Marius decided to seize that position, but failed to reckon with the complex tactical challenges that the site presented; his eventual success was determined more by good fortune than by his valour and skill. In Sallust's account, it was only the solitary attempt of a Ligurian soldier, a member of the auxiliary troops that fought in the Roman army, to climb the wall of the fort; a holm oak (*ilex*) that happened to stick from the wall gave him the support that made his rise possible; he then looked into the walls and enabled his comrades to enter the compound from a side that was not well defended. That individual act of single-handed, hazardous bravery enabled Marius' troops to make a breakthrough and have the upper hand over the resistance of the population.

Sallust's account is the only reasonably full narrative of this phase of the conflict that has come down to us, and there is no serious reason to disbelieve the main contention that it makes on the quality and effectiveness of Marius' leadership. It is important, however, to recognize the literary effect that Sallust is keen to pursue, here and elsewhere in his work. As ever, he is interested in elegant and geometric correspondences within his text. Marius is a flawed leader, who has nonetheless made a contribution to the Roman war effort that Metellus was not capable of making; in turn, the strategic ability that Marius lacks is soon to be found in another figure that steps onto the stage of the conflict.

The consul was soon joined by his quaestor L. Cornelius Sulla (138–78 BC), who had been busy with levy operations in Latium and Italy in the previous months and had brought to Africa a cavalry contingent. The differences between the two men must have been obvious to their contemporaries. Sulla hailed from a distinguished patrician family, although the last of his ancestors to have certainly held public office was his grandfather, who was praetor in 186 BC; he was considerably younger and less experienced than the consul, and had just started to make his way up the *cursus honorum*. Unlike Marius, he did not have any hesitations in displaying his knowledge of Greek and Roman literature, and in showing his willingness to enjoy the pleasures of life. He was, however, a very capable man, equally gifted in the art of political dissimulation and in the difficult craft of gaining the sympathy of his soldiers without diminishing his own gravitas. Such, at least, is the portrait of Sallust, who talks of Sulla with hindsight, in the full knowledge of his later career. Sulla is portrayed as bringing new forces to the campaign. Perhaps for this reason Sallust makes the dubious claim that he had no military experience: this can hardly be the case, since Marius had entrusted him with a task of such considerable significance as the levy of the troops at a critical junction of the campaign.

Moreover, if Sallust is to be believed, Sulla was apparently respectful of the prerogatives of the consul and of his leading role in the campaign. Marius gave further proofs of his leadership ability in responding to a sudden attack launched by Jugurtha and his ally and father-in-law, the local dynast Bocchus, as the Roman troops were approaching their winter quarters. He gave proof of a cool-headed and robust leadership, and of his ability to defend his men while at the same time launching the attack against the enemy; he apparently retained control over the infantry, while Sulla was in charge of the cavalry. The fighting continued until night fell; Marius then placed his camp in the vicinity of a source; at the break of dawn he launched a successful attack on the enemy troops that proved decisive. It was the most considerable military breakthrough in the campaign until that moment. As the army resumed its march to winter quarters, the leadership of Marius appeared stronger than ever: his presence in the ranks was constantly felt by the soldiers, and he would make a point of following their actions and sharing in their toils. As Sallust points out, in that campaign Marius managed to retain the discipline of his soldiers by instilling a sense of honour in them, rather than enforcing a strict code of conduct: in doing so, he appeared to be loyal to the values and practices of his youth.

Sulla showed the same skills and the same mindset: when the armies met for another confrontation in the vicinity of Cirta, he took part directly in the cavalry attack on the Mauri, and joined in the subsequent military action. The attack was not as successful as expected. Marius had to intervene personally to rescue his cavalry. After that victory against Jugurtha and Bocchus, Marius' army could reach Cirta, where he was planning to winter his troops: with hindsight, Sallust notes that there was no doubt about the fact that victory was in hand for Rome. Many contemporaries will have surely reached the same conclusion. Shortly after his arrival at Cirta, Marius was approached by Bocchus, the closest ally of the king, with a request to send him two envoys, so that they could confer about their mutual interests. It was the offer of an underhand deal: Marius, who must have been keen to remain in control of the army and plan future operations, entrusted the talks to Sulla and another aide, Aulus Manlius. The task of setting out the conditions to Bocchus fell upon Sulla. He could rely on the generosity of the Roman people, after having experienced its might, if he was prepared to end his connection with Jugurtha. Bocchus readily accepted the offer. Some of his advisers, allegedly bribed by Jugurtha, tried to persuade him to reconsider his choice, but to no avail. The further success of Marius' troops in the siege of a small fort held by Jugurtha in the desert must have confirmed his view that the destiny of the war was a foregone conclusion. He sent envoys to the Roman winter quarters to agree a comprehensive agreement. After being attacked and robbed by some Gaetulian robbers, they were received by Sulla, who displayed towards them the same generosity that he displayed to the soldiers shortly after his arrival in Africa: a distinctive feature of his public conduct that had significant political implications. It was not hard for Sulla to reach an agreement with them, which was in turn confirmed by the talks they had with Marius, who met them in Utica at the end of his foray into the desert.

The meeting with the envoys of Bocchus, however, was not just a matter for the consul to deal with: he made sure to summon all the members of his staff, including Sulla, and all the senators that were in the province. Even a well-regarded and influential figure like Marius could not afford to disregard the customary practice and did not refrain from seeking advice from his peers. In fact, the aim of the debate that Marius led was not even that of deciding whether to accept the peace terms or not, but whether to allow the envoys of Bocchus to sail to Rome and seek an audience with the Senate. It was for the Senate to decide on all the matters pertaining to foreign policy and the main directions of provincial administration. That principle had been in operation throughout the mid-Republican period, and not even Marius, the new man, was prepared to disregard it, or to suggest an alternative course of action. The five envoys of Bocchus parted ways: two returned to Bocchus, whom they informed of the developments and especially of Sulla's benevolence, and three went to Rome, where they sought and obtained (after being reminded of Bocchus' previous misdemeanours) the pardon of the Roman people. The alliance, however, would be granted to him depending on Bocchus' future conduct.

The terms of the conversations between Marius and the Senate ahead of the audience with the ambassadors remain beyond our reach. What is certain is that the response of the senators was of direct help to the solution of the war. It gave a clear hint to Bocchus that his direct support would be needed to defeat Jugurtha, and the king took it. He addressed a message to Marius, asking for Sulla to be sent to him for talks. The quaestor made his way, accompanied by a robust contingent that included a number of auxiliary troops from Italy and Spain: a display of the military might of the Roman army, and a precautionary measure too. That there were some lingering concerns about Bocchus' real attitude is confirmed by the anxiety suffered by the Romans when Volux, the son of Bocchus, appeared on the horizon, with a robust escort of knights. The Roman soldiers started to get ready for battle, until Volux made his peaceful intentions clear and accompanied Sulla and his retinue to his father, as he had been instructed to do. When the night fell and the cortège had to stop and set up camp, Volux warned Sulla that Jugurtha's army was approaching; Sulla agreed to move the troops at daybreak, hoping to continue his march without having to escape. Yet, he received the news that Jugurtha was barely two miles away. Moments of tension ensued, with the Roman soldiers openly suspecting Volux of having arranged an ambush. Sulla confronted him and nearly expelled him from the camp, but was eventually persuaded by Volux to march through Jugurtha's ranks: Volux's presence would have been sufficient to persuade the Numidian king not to harm him. The plan presented a huge risk, but proved successful.

That turn of events shows that Bocchus was still, at least from a formal point of view, reasonably close to Jugurtha, who was aware of the imminent talks with Sulla, and made sure to send one of his envoys, Aspar, to Bocchus just when the Romans were about to reach him. That precaution was not sufficient: Sulla and Bocchus made sure to meet privately at night, after holding a perfunctory meeting before

Jugurtha's envoy. According to Sallust's memorable summary of those fateful talks, Bocchus offered his unconditional loyalty to Rome and asked for his loyalty to be put to the test; Sulla disdainfully replied that the only way in which Bocchus could please the Romans, who had defeated him in battle, was to do something more advantageous for them than for himself. That is a striking illustration of the primacy of the strongest. The gist of the request was strikingly at odds with the principles and practice of Roman *fides*, good faith, a principle that was often invoked in Roman foreign policy: he asked for Bocchus to arrange the capture of Jugurtha. Bocchus accepted the request; he then started talks with Jugurtha's envoy, ostensibly to convey to the king the news that the Romans were prepared to negotiate a peace; in turn, he received a request to arrange the capture of Marius. Even Sallust seems uncertain on the actual motives of Bocchus at that moment, and does not rule out the possibility that he was genuinely uncertain about which choice to make. He eventually decided to enable the capture of Jugurtha, having made sure to arrange a meeting with him in the presence of a few lightly armed men.

Sulla had therefore secured the felicitous conclusion of the conflict with Jugurtha. The credit for that victory, however, went fully to Marius, to whom Sulla duly surrendered the king. The success on the African front was a substantial achievement, although it came later than Marius had promised in placing his bid for the consulship of 108. The news of his victory reached Rome when a new major crisis was looming on the city: the consular armies deployed in Gaul had been defeated by the Teutones. As Sallust points out, everybody's hopes converged on Marius, who was elected to the consulship for the year 104 despite being absent from Rome: an extraordinary development, which revealed the degree of confidence that voters had in him. 'All the hopes and resources of the city rested in him': Sallust's remark in the last sentence of the *Jugurthine War* implies that those were soon due to be betrayed.

The Germanic War

The development of the war against the Germanic invaders had been intertwined with the final part of the Jugurthine conflict, and with a wider difficulty of Rome to make substantial progress beyond the Alps. In 107 BC the consul L. Cassius Longinus fought a campaign in Aquitania, in Transalpine Gaul, and suffered a crushing defeat at the hands of the Tigurini, a Celtic community, losing his life in battle. His legate C. Popillius Laenas negotiated an agreement that saved the lives of a large number of Roman soldiers, but was regarded as unacceptable in Rome, and led to a prosecution against him by the tribune C. Coelius. Laenas was tried before the people and sentenced to exile. In October 105 the consul Cn. Mallius Maximus and Q. Servilius Caepio (*cos.* 106) led another campaign in Southern Gaul, with a view to addressing the advance of the Teutones into the region. Their army met a major debacle at Arausio (modern Orange), which was the greatest Roman defeat since that suffered against Hannibal at Cannae more than a century earlier, in 216. Things were made even worse by the reports that Caepio had stolen gold from a sacred treasure that belonged to allies of the Roman people. He was prosecuted shortly afterwards, again under the initiative of a tribune of the plebs. Reports reached Rome with news of the defeat, as well as disquieting news about the size of the enemy forces, which were reported to be in the region of 300,000 men. As Plutarch makes clear, the most disturbing feature of that threat was not just the military strength of the troops, but the fact that they were accompanied by women and children, and were looking for land in Italy in which to settle permanently. Traditions about the descent of the Gauls into Italy and their legendary victories against the Etruscans were revived. The Teutones were, in fact, poorly known enemies, with whom Rome had no previous dealings. The war was regarded as a major challenge, which questioned the very survival of the city.

The defeat at Arausio prompted a robust reaction. The consul P. Rutilius Rufus reportedly introduced stronger standards of discipline across the part of the army that was under his command. A part of the tradition, no doubt influenced by Rutilius' own autobiographical work, readily establishes a link between Rutilius' intervention and the later development of the campaign. What appears to have played an even more significant role, however, is the general change of the political climate in Rome. Q. Servilius Caepio was stripped of his command by a vote of the people; in the following year a law was passed whereby those who had been deprived of their *imperium* were to lose their senatorial status. The consul who was also implicated with the defeat, Cn. Mallius, was also at the centre of a serious controversy, and the proposal to send him to exile was tabled. More importantly, however, there was a strong call to entrust the leadership of the campaign to the man who had just obtained a long-awaited success on the African front. It is quite possible that, as Plutarch points out, the sentiment against the *nobiles* that had accompanied the election of Marius in 108 was rekindled on that occasion. The election of Marius to the consulship for the year 104 was in breach of the legislation on office-holding, which set clear rules on the number of years that had to intervene before one could be allowed to hold the same post; moreover, it ran against the established practice whereby the candidacy to a magistracy had to be placed in person at Rome.

After returning to Rome with the bulk of the army that had defeated Jugurtha, Marius took office on the first day of the year, and before setting off on campaign he duly celebrated the triumph for his victory in Africa. The procession of the army, led by the victorious general, from the outskirts of Rome along the *via Triumphalis*, all the way up to the Capitoline Hill, was a major public celebration and a complex religious ritual. It also had at its very core the emphatic display of the booty generated by the campaign – including the prisoners that had been taken, first and foremost the defeated king. Plutarch offers a striking portrayal of the king as he is being carried in chains, and ends up losing his mind: when he is brought into the *carcer Mamertinum*, the jailhouse of the city of Rome, he has an earlobe torn off by a jailer who wants to seize his golden earring, is thrown into a cesspit, and starves to death six days later.

Public attention, however, was focused on what was happening outside the prison, on the stage of Roman politics. Some regarded with concern the behaviour of Marius in the immediate aftermath of the triumph, when he entered the venue on the Capitol where the Senate was gathered wearing his triumphal robe: conduct that ran against established practice and did not fail to attract controversy. Marius was quick to sense the mood in the Senate and to respond appropriately: he readily changed into the *toga praetexta* that curule magistrates customarily wore. That episode, however, did not alter the fact that Marius was the obvious candidate for the command in the campaign: his colleague in the consulship, C. Flavius Fimbria (himself a new man) did not have a comparable military record, and not even his political enemies argued against that. Marius was formally assigned the command, probably after another vote of the *comitia*, and began to recruit and train his army, reportedly enforcing standards of discipline and labour that had hardly even been matched. If we are to believe a story retold by Plutarch, the rigour of Marius did not stop even before his nephew C. Lusius, when it emerged that he had been sexually harassing one of his soldiers. Marius could also rely on an important tactical advantage. He did not have to lead his army right into a military confrontation with the enemies, but could enjoy some respite when it emerged that the main aim of the enemy, at least in the short term, was not Italy, but Spain. He therefore had longer to prepare for the later phase of the conflict.

The prospect of a Germanic attack on Italy, however, remained very realistic and was apparently the crucial factor in determining the election of Marius to a third consulship in a row for the following year. The coming of the enemy was expected for the spring. As was the case at other junctions of Roman history, the breach of established constitutional practice in the previous year had made the election of Marius to a third term in office come across as a less problematic solution than the mere extension of the Gallic command that he had received a few months earlier. Yet, the open confrontation with the enemy was not quite imminent. Marius even had to return to Rome during the summer to preside over the consular elections for the following year, after the sudden death of his colleague L. Aurelius Orestes. It is unclear what other business took up his term in office, except for the continuation of the preparation of the campaign: it is surprising, for example, not to find any evidence for legislative production actively supported by Marius in these years. One source records a bill of the tribune L. Appuleius Saturninus, who sought 'the favour of Marius' soldiers' by putting forward a proposal for land assignments in North Africa. His fellow-tribune Baebius vetoed the proposal, but Saturninus had him stoned to death by the mob. Marius' position on this issue is nowhere recorded, and it is perhaps significant that the source for Saturninus' bill (the biographical epitome *De viris illustribus*, probably dating to the mid-first century AD) states that the tribune did not seek the favour of Marius, but that of his soldiers. On the other hand, it is unlikely that a proposal of that nature could have been put forward without Marius' consent, if not active involvement, and it is tempting to see a link between the enlisting of *proletarii* for the Jugurthine War and the prospect of land assignments for the veterans of the campaign. The scale on which Saturninus' law was implemented, however, is impossible to establish.

Plutarch notes that the field of candidates to the consulship for the following year was stronger than had been the case in the previous years, but Marius could rely on the support of an influential advocate. The tribune Saturninus, who could already rely on the widespread support of political support among the Roman populace, publicly made the case in favour of his re-election. Although Marius publicly stated his unwillingness to stand for office again, there was little doubt that the stand taken by Saturninus had been previously agreed with him, and was the symptom of a newly forged political alliance. The partnership between the prominent general and the vocal tribune was to become one of the great political developments of the following years, and was probably regarded with concern by some from the outset. Plutarch takes the opportunity to point out that Saturninus' advocacy in favour of Marius was blatant and undignified. At any rate, the operation was successful: Marius was elected to the consulship for the year 102. His colleague was Q. Lutatius Catulus, who had lost a number of consular elections in the previous years, and could rely (if one is to believe Plutarch's highly schematic account) on support within the Senate and among the people alike. Later in life Catulus wrote an autobiographical work that no longer survives, but did not fail to make an impact on the ancient tradition on this period, and cast a hostile light on Marius.

After that third consecutive election Marius devoted all his energies to the campaign. The focus of the war was beyond the Alps. The Teutones had descended into the Iberian peninsula, but their march was put to an end by a crushing defeat against the Celtiberians, and they resumed their march along the coast of the Mediterranean back into Southern Gaul. That is where Marius reached them: he set up camp along the river Rhône and took care of a complex system of logistical supplies to the army. He also took care of major works at the mouth of the Rhône, which had no direct bearings on his campaign, but was a good opportunity to keep his men busy before the start of the operations. The fullest account of the campaign may be found in Plutarch. It is based on the assumption – which is not corroborated in the surviving evidence – that the 'barbarians', the Germanic enemies of Rome, were following a shared strategy, and had divided their movements across different fronts: on their alleged plan, the Teutones were to march from coastal Iberia to Liguria, in north-west Italy, while the Cimbri were to move from Noricum (roughly corresponding to modern Austria) into the Po Valley and north-east and central Italy. The Teutones proved very keen to take action, and were supported by the strength of their number; the tone with which Plutarch describes their military prowess is tinged with the fascination that the stuff of legend commands. However, the fundamental point on the development of the campaign must surely be retained: Marius' strategic choice was to meet the enemies in Southern Gaul, well before they could cross into Italy.

In Plutarch's account Marius is not overly keen to embark on an open, full-scale military confrontation. The Teutones surrounded the fortified camp and called him to a pitched battle, but his reaction was to restrain his soldiers and ask them to observe the enemy from the watchtowers. Such a choice prompted irritation and puzzlement among the soldiers, and allegations against Marius did start to circulate among them and eventually reached the commander: some even went as far as accusing him of cowardice. Far from irritating Marius, they pleased him. Plutarch does not hesitate to depict him as a shrewd, manipulative leader who is prepared to play mind-games with his own soldiers if he feels that it could serve the wider aims of the campaign. It is not about a moral judgement: quite the contrary, it is a recognition of his resolve and clarity of purpose. Later readers of Plutarch did not fail to see the importance of that point. Machiavelli, in his *Discourses on Livy's First Decade* (3.37), emphatically praised the tactical intelligence of that decision, which put Marius' soldiers in the best position to launch a successful attack shortly afterwards. His aim was to enable his soldiers to get used to the presence of the enemy and to gradually feel less daunted by it. The plan was successful, according to Plutarch: the jibes and verbal challenges that the Teutones would shout from their positions, well within hearing distance from the Roman camp, increased the resolve of the Roman soldiers.

Marius, predictably enough, did not use this argument with his soldiers, but invoked an important religious consideration. He claimed that some oracles had given him an indication of the time and place of his future victory, and he was waiting for the right opportunity. The implications that this prophecy could have on the troops' morale are obvious: it implied the promise of success to come. Inspired prophecies, however, were usually not part of the mainstream religious tradition in Rome. As far as we know, it was not customary for a Roman commander to present his soldiers with predictions of the future along those lines. The general was, as a serving magistrate, closely involved with the performance of important religious rituals that were intended to secure the favour of the gods, but did not typically involve the production of prophecies, which were usually avoided in the mainstream practice of Roman public religion. Indeed, Marius appeared to owe his special prophetic knowledge to a foreign diviner. Since the beginning of the campaign he had on his retinue a Syrian woman called Martha, who would also give him instruction on when to perform sacrifices to the gods. Martha had come into contact with Marius through a convoluted process, which reveals something about the way in which religious knowledge in Republican Rome was circulated and controlled. Martha first sought to present her prophecies to the Senate, but was denied an audience. She then succeeded in presenting her predictions to some women of the nobility, including Marius' wife. She eventually met, and earned the admiration of, the consul through the mediation of his wife. What is striking is that Marius did not strive to conceal his connection with the priestess, in the same way in which a modern politician who routinely consults a fortune teller would probably keep quiet about such a habit. On the contrary, Martha was openly allowed to follow Marius on campaign: she was carried in a litter and would attend the sacrifices wearing very distinctive attire. That behaviour was baffling to many, and some did speculate that his apparent enthusiasm for the priestess's lore was merely a posture.

Whatever Marius' own motives might have been, it is beyond doubt that the presence of Martha on the campaign was the symptom of an exceptionally tense moment, in which religious concerns played a distinctive role. A number of signs of divine favour or displeasure were noticed and reported in various parts of Italy. Most impressively, the priests in charge of the cult of Mater Magna (Great Mother) in the sanctuary of Pessinus in Asia Minor – a cult that had been introduced within the body of Roman public religion in 205 – announced to the Senate that the goddess had predicted the imminent victory of the Romans. The Senate immediately took heed of that extraordinary prophecy by decreeing that a temple be dedicated to the goddess after the victory. Martha's prophetic craft, therefore, was not the only kind of Eastern lore that appeared to assert the victory of Marius. But such divinatory expertise was regarded by some as a threat. Bataces, the priest of Mater Magna, did not just obtain an audience with the Senate; he also asked to present the response of the goddess to a popular assembly. The tribune A. Postumius used his power of veto to prevent him from addressing the people. According to Plutarch, Postumius died shortly afterwards, and his sudden demise was widely regarded as evidence for the reliability of the prophecy that he had tried to stop. The background of his action is too little known to allow an informed conclusion on its significance. It may be read as evidence that Marius still had vocal and effective opponents in Rome, even within the tribunician college, or it may be a reflection of a more general concern to maintain the control of religious knowledge, including prophetic expertise, within the political elite.

The circulation of disturbing divine signs and more or less specific prophecies on the outcome of the war appear to have had hardly any impact on the conflict, although it is very likely that they did affect the morale of Marius' army. Marius' men had kept their position in the fortified camp that had been set at the beginning of the campaign; the Teutones launched an attack against them, with a view to overcoming their opposition and continuing their march towards the Alps. Marius let them pass through, only to lead his army outside the camp and chase the enemy until he caught up with them at Aquae Sextiae (modern Aix-en-Provence). He then set up a new camp there, despite the reluctance of his soldiers, who were especially concerned with access to water supply. The first open military confrontation of the enemy started precisely from the need to access water. Some camp servants of the Romans went to a river nearby and took the chance to attack an enemy contingent that happened to be in the area. The clash soon escalated into a full-blown confrontation between the Ambrones – a community that had already fought alongside the Teutones in the battle of Arausio – and the Ligurians, who were fighting as an auxiliary contingent within the Roman army. Surprisingly enough, the Ligurians claimed to share the same ethnic origin as the Ambrones, but that did not prevent them from taking the field against them. A Roman contingent soon came in support, and in turn the women of the Ambrones rushed to the scene and tried to prevent the defeat of their men, which by that point must have seemed a foregone conclusion. Plutarch offers a memorable depiction of the staunch resistance that they presented to the winning Roman troops, 'their fierce spirits unvanquished to the end'.

The account of this military confrontation is not just an exercise that serves Plutarch's narrative and literary needs remarkably well. It also draws attention to one of the fundamental features of the literary tradition on the war. Much as Marius was the Roman general that led the campaign and eventually won it, his role in the crucial stages of the war is marginal. He played no part, most notably, in causing that first military confrontation and he apparently failed to predict the arrival of a larger contingent of Teutones – which was soon joined by the survivors among the Ambrones – in the vicinity of the Roman camp. The position of the Romans was somewhat supported by the hasty decision of the Teutones to start battle before being on equal terms with the enemy; Marius, conversely, made the sensible decision to exploit the strategic advantage of being on favourable ground and to instruct his soldiers to wait for the enemies' attack. When that came, the Romans were in a position to bring the enemy lines into disarray by leading a double line of attack with the support of Marius' legate M. Claudius Marcellus. The measure of the Roman success is conveyed by the wholly implausible figure that Plutarch gives for the number of prisoners captured on the day – in excess of 100,000. An impressive amount of booty was also seized. The material rewards of the victory of Aquae Sextiae are crudely conveyed by two anecdotal notices: the soil of the neighbouring city was made considerably more fertile by the decomposition of the corpses on the battlefield, and the bones of the fallen were used as fences of the vineyards in the territory of neighbouring Massalia (modern Marseilles). Moreover, the size of the booty that was gathered at the end of the campaign could lead to anticipate a lavish triumph upon the army's return to Rome. The anticipation of the celebration that awaited them in Rome and of the material rewards that victory entailed predictably corroborated the relationship of the soldiers with Marius and their commitment to him. The message that Marius had been elected to a fifth consulship for the following year reached him as he was celebrating the victory with his soldiers in a ceremony that Plutarch describes as a peculiar military and sacrificial act.

Plutarch frames this moment as a powerful illustration of a familiar historical principle, the inextricable coexistence of good and bad fortune, and of joy and sorrow in human affairs. Marius' comprehensive victory in Transalpine Gaul was accompanied by a major Roman defeat in Cisalpine Gaul, where his fellow consul Catulus had failed to contain the descent into Italy of the Cimbri. Plutarch (who is no doubt basing some of his information on Catulus' autobiographical work) points out that he was concerned not to divide his forces into a number of fronts: that reasonable concern prevented him from opposing adequate resistance to the might of the attackers. He tried to put a river, the Atiso (probably to be identified with the Adige, in north-east Italy) between himself and the enemy, effectively turning it into a natural barrier against the invaders. The plan did not come to terms with the resilience of the Cimbri to the cold Alpine winter and the strength of their attack. They just stormed against the defences created by Catulus and compelled the majority of the Roman troops to flee the camp that Catulus had set. It was, by all intents and purposes, a hasty retreat. Catulus endeavoured to make it come across as a tactical move, and took the lead of the army. He opposed more resistance to the descent of the Cimbri further south, but the attack into Italy was now in full steam. Catulus had conducted himself worthily, if we are to believe Plutarch, but had failed to make a substantial impact on the campaign, and Marius was summoned to Rome by the Senate to discuss the situation. His conduct is depicted as that of a selfless statesman: he refused to celebrate the triumph that he had been granted by the Senate, and he readily agreed to lead a new campaign by joining forces with Catulus. He therefore summoned his troops from Transalpine Gaul and led them to Cisalpine Gaul, with a view to confronting the enemy in the Po Valley. By that point the Cimbri were reluctant to take on the challenge: they were apparently awaiting the arrival of the Teutones from Gaul. They then had talks with Marius in which they demanded land for themselves, only for their request to be denied by Marius, who showed them the king of the Teutones, whom he had captured in Gaul, in chains.

The momentum of the war was back with the Romans, or, at least, Marius was not interested in pursuing a peaceful solution before obtaining a major victory against the Cimbri. The decisive military confrontation took place at a site called Campi Raudii, near Vercellae, almost certainly located in the neighbourhood of modern Vercelli in north-west Italy (although some scholars have placed it in north-east Italy, in the Po Delta region, between Rovigo and Ferrara). The site of the battle was agreed upon by the two parties, and gave the margin to the Romans to deploy their cavalry and to the Cimbri the opportunity to make the most of their large numbers. The ensuing battle was a major event, which involved the participation of two Roman armies under two different commanders of the same rank. Catulus provided an account of it in his memoirs, and Plutarch's reconstruction of the battle is strongly influenced by it. It is apparent that he was determined to downplay the merits of Marius in the conduct of the battle, and that he argued that Marius had himself given a disingenuous representation of how events had unfolded. The extent of their disagreement reflects the importance of the battle. Sulla also took part, under Catulus' command, and discussed its development in his own memoirs. He pointed out that the decisive moment of the battle was determined by the sudden appearance of a cloud of dust, which prevented Marius from assessing the position of the enemy, and by the effect that the intense heat of the summer day on which the battle took place had on the Cimbri. Catulus also emphasized the fact that his soldiers were apparently unaffected by the summer temperature.

The Roman attack, whether determined by Marius' lucid strategic vision or by fortuitous developments, had a devastating impact on the enemy. The Cimbrian women came to the rescue of their men and shared their tragic destiny; a similar scene had occurred at Aquae Sextiae. Plutarch does not spare gory details. It was by all accounts a major victory for Rome. Intense disagreement on the factors that determined it and on who was to be credited with it continued after the events, started in the hours following the victory. While the property of the enemy was taken to Marius' camp, Catulus got hold of the standards and the official spoils; a difference that Catulus used to corroborate his claim over the victory. The controversy was so intense that some citizens from the colony of Parma, who had served in the Roman army, were instructed to resolve the dispute. They went through the bodies of the fallen enemies to establish whether most of them had been killed by the weapons of Catulus' soldiers or by those of Marius' men.

Whatever the outcome of that arbitration might have been, the consensus in Rome on who was to be credited with the defeat of the Cimbri was clear. According to Plutarch, upon his return Marius was even hailed as the third founder of Rome, after Romulus, and Camillus, the legendary leader who had averted the Gallic invasion of 390 BC. By rescuing the city from a likely disaster he had effectively offered it a new lease of life, and deserved suitable recognition for his achievements. It was an extraordinary claim to make, and Plutarch's evidence is not immune from problems. It also gives no insight into the extent to which Marius played a direct role in shaping the wider perception of his own achievements. It is a safe guess that some of his associates, quite probably also Saturninus, did extol his merits to the Roman people. The credit that was attributed to him was the symptom of a new political climate. The extent to which the achievements of Marius were celebrated placed him in a domain that was not quite comparable to that of any of his contemporaries. Although speaking of a straightforward process of 'deification' in Rome is hardly helpful, and the boundaries between men and gods were generally understood in different terms from what is the case in monotheistic contexts, some of the honours that Marius received are closely comparable to those received by the gods: he was presented for instance with offerings of food and libations. Such a lavish tribute also had a clear political implication: calls were made for Marius to be allowed to celebrate the triumphs for his victories against the Teutones and the Cimbri alone, and for Catulus not to be granted such privilege. Marius made a point of sharing his triumph with Catulus, partly to convey a measure of his restraint, and partly (as Plutarch argues, perhaps developing a suggestion from Catulus) out of fear of the hostile reaction of Catulus' soldiers, had their commander being excluded from the triumph. Ruling out Catulus from the major celebration that marked the successful end of the conflict would not just involve a negative judgement on the commander, but would also reflect negatively on his army. It was also a political choice that had, in turn, major religious implications.

Whether Marius actually feared the consequences of denying Catulus a triumph is a matter for speculation. The very fact that the suggestion was made (whether at the time, or by later, informed students of the period) is a symptom of the deep tensions that marred Roman politics at the time, and of the rife potential for instability, and indeed full-scale violence in the city. However, Marius' chief interest at the time was not to foment further tensions, but to gather consensus on his name, as he was about to put forward his candidacy for a sixth consulship.

The revenues of the Germanic campaign also enabled a further, remarkable, development, which is overlooked by most of the literary sources. Upon his return Marius promoted the construction and dedication of a temple of Honos and Virtus, 'Honour and Manly Valour': no archaeological traces survive of this sanctuary, but the references that Vitruvius makes to it in his treatise on architecture (written between 27 and 23 BC) leave one in no doubt what an ambitious project it was from a structural and artistic standpoint. Cicero mentions it as a venue for a Senate session in the mid-first century BC. The choice to dedicate a temple to two 'abstract' deities which were closely connected to values that played a major role in the Roman political discourse, and were of obvious interest to a man with a strong military profile like Marius, is also remarkable. They also show that a new phase in Marius' career was beginning: after achieving a remarkable military record, he set out to establish himself as a major presence in the political and religious landscape of the city. The proceeds of the Germanic victory put him in good stead for that, but considerable challenges awaited him. For the first time in his career, he was not in a position to seek political and electoral support on the basis of his ability to address a military emergency. He had to seek votes on the basis of his political credentials, and to seek the consensus of the Roman people through an election campaign. He needed to muster a very different set of skills from what he had displayed until then. The following years are, to a large extent, the story of his failure to adapt to a very different context from the one in which he had built his unrivalled reputation.

3

Marius' Fall

The wrong crowd

It would be misguided to regard Marius' decision to stand for the consulship of 100 BC as a straightforward symptom of unbridled personal ambition, much as that is what Plutarch would have us believe. There were important political steps to be taken. The focus of Plutarch's discussion is consistently on Marius' character, as it is to be expected of a discussion that is chiefly focused on the moral dimension. The account of his fifth consulship is very unsatisfactory indeed in this respect: the focus is on the consequences that ambition had on his leadership ability and on his interaction with the people, which proved to be far less effective in peacetime than had been the case on the campaigns that he led over the years. However, Plutarch also argues that Marius had to seek the support of the populace in order to overcome the limits of the annual magistracy that he held, and which back in Rome was no longer associated with a military commitment. For this reason – so argues the biographer – Marius chose to launch a violent attack against the nobility, and especially one of its figureheads, Metellus Numidicus, the consul of 109, with whom he had by then a deep-seated personal enmity, and with whom he had conducted himself ungratefully at a crucial junction of the war in Numidia. Metellus intended to stand against Marius for a new consulship for 100 BC; in Plutarch's narrative, Marius' fear of him is the factor that turns him onto the wrong path, and changes him into a nemesis of Marius. It is because of the need to oppose Metellus that

Marius chose questionable allies such as Saturninus, started to resort to demagogic arguments, and even used illegal methods to increase his electoral support: first by granting citizenship to a large number of soldiers from Camerinum who had fought under his standards, and secondly by bribing voters in Rome, immediately before the election. It is noteworthy that Plutarch is here using a contemporary source, the autobiography of Rutilius Rufus, although that is of course no guarantee of reliable information: Rutilius was a personal foe and a committed political opponent of Marius.

The effort paid off. Metellus was defeated and Marius was elected to the consulship of 100 along with a colleague on whose loyalty he could apparently rely, L. Valerius Flaccus. Marius was, after that sixth electoral victory, at the centre of a political coalition to which he owed his recent success. The tribune L. Appuleius Saturninus and the praetor C. Servilius Glaucia were political forces with which he had to come to terms. Glaucia had been a vocal political figure in the preceding years, had attracted hostility and controversy on the part of the senatorial elite, and had escaped the expulsion from the Senate under the censorship of Q. Caecilius Metellus in 102. After holding the tribunate and the praetorship in consecutive years, he intended to place his bid for the consulship for 99: that would have required an exception be made on established practice. Saturninus was a remarkable public speaker and held the tribunate at various times. He had a complex and highly ambitious political agenda. His focus was not just on an agrarian law that provided for Marius' veterans. He also drew up a new corn law, a measure that restricted the powers of the magistrates in the provinces, and probably a piece of legislation dealing with provincial administration in the East. Saturninus was not just a shrewd political agitator: his policies show a degree of ambition that had not been matched since the day of Gaius Gracchus. He was also prepared to make use of violence to support his strategy. During the tribunician elections he did not hesitate to order the assassination of Aulus Nonius (or Nunnius), a rival for the same office who stood a very good chance of election. The opposition of just one member of the tribunician college could be sufficient to stop all the plans of Saturninus and his associates, and the decision to get rid of Nonius shows that there was no intention to take any chances.

As Appian's account of the agrarian bill makes clear, the focus of Saturninus' proposal was the provision of land to the veterans of Marius. It is beyond doubt that the project had the direct support of the consul; in fact, it is likely that Marius had played a significant role in shaping its contents. The reasons why the bill was put forward as a proposal of a tribune, rather than as one of the consul, are at best the object of informed speculation. It is conceivable that Marius did not have a sufficient support base in the city of Rome, and that he regarded the powerful advocacy of a tribune as a major asset. The link between tribunes and agrarian laws dated back to the age of the Gracchi, and would have therefore placed that proposal within the framework of *popularis* politics – i.e., within a very clear political tradition. It is also possible that he felt that the proposal would have greater chances of success if he somewhat distanced himself from it, since the bill included clauses that were unquestionably favourable to his own interests: indeed, according to Plutarch, Marius even spoke against the bill in the Senate, in an extreme exercise of political dissimulation – one of the many in his life, according to a hostile strand of the tradition. If that reading is correct, we would then be confronted with a symptom of Marius' relative weakness in a political context that remained fragmented and competitive in equal measure.

If we want to get a sense of the terms of Saturninus' bill, we need to look beyond Plutarch, who mentions it in the space of a few lines, and turn to the account that Appian gave of it in his narrative of the Republican civil wars. The bill is framed within a narrative that puts at the centre the link between economic and social instability across Italy, political division in Rome, and the emergence of a cycle of political violence that will eventually lead the Republic to a sorry end. The treatment of the events of 100 BC follows without break of continuity from the discussion of the death of Gaius Gracchus: it is opened by the assassination of a lawfully elected tribune, Nonius, by Saturninus and Glaucia, and the subsequent cover-up masterminded by the two agitators and by Marius, who shared with them a bitter hostility towards Caecilius Metellus. The precedent of the Gracchi was very clear to the minds of Saturninus and his men: one of them was a certain L. Equitius, who even claimed to be the natural son of Tiberius Gracchus, although he was publicly denounced as an impostor by Sempronia, the only surviving sister of the Gracchi.

According to Appian, the law provided for the allocation and distribution among Marius' veterans of the land that had been conquered during the campaign against the Cimbri – presumably in Northern Italy. Another source, the elusive biographical work *On illustrious men*, gives a different account of the scope of the bill in a brief biography of Saturninus, and mentions land assignments in Sicily and Greece; it also refers to *noui coloni*, 'new colonists', strongly suggesting that the foundation of new settlements was envisaged. This work, as we have seen, is also the only source for the land bill that Saturninus put forward in 103. Whatever the scope and impact of Saturninus' proposals might have been, there was an important difference from the agrarian laws put forward by the Gracchi. While those provided for the needs of the landless poor, these measures addressed the needs of the veterans. It is true that Marius' army included men who had no property qualification whatsoever, and that the envisaged project therefore served the interests of some individuals that could fairly be deemed to be 'poor'. The logic of the reform, however, was altogether different from the projects of the Gracchi. On the other hand, an aspect of the project has a level of similarity with an initiative of Tiberius Gracchus. The law included measures on how the land assignments would be funded, and stated that the gold that Caepio had illegally seized at Tolosa (modern Toulouse) in Narbonese Gaul would be used to purchase land. Three decades earlier, Tiberius Gracchus had unsuccessfully proposed to use the revenues of the new province of Asia to fund his agrarian law. The principle that the reform had to be funded from resources to be drawn from other sectors of society was being upheld by Saturninus as it had been by Gracchus, albeit in very different terms.

That the bill was intended to serve the interests of Marius and his army is made clear beyond reasonable doubt by a brief reference in a later speech of Cicero, who points out that under Saturninus' law Marius was allowed to grant Roman citizenship to three citizens of each Roman colony: a remarkable provision, which also suggests that Marius was supposed to travel extensively across the Italian peninsula, and probably to follow the enforcement of the reform very closely. The hostile slant of the tradition suggests that the proponents of the reform were prepared to be ruthless to secure its success. After getting rid of Nonius, who could have vetoed the bill, they included a clause that required senators to swear an oath to abide by whatever the people would choose to vote. The main aim of this move was to make sure that no future legal or political challenge be brought against the validity of the law, or indeed against aspects of its implementation. Failure to take the oath would have entailed a fine. The political rationale that underlay this requirement was of course of even wider import: it implied a clear view of the balance of power between people and Senate.

However, it would be misguided to think that the *people* were unanimously backing the reform: on the contrary, many in Rome were hostile to the law, because they felt that the Italians would unduly benefit from it. Similar tensions had arisen in the age of the Gracchi, who relied on firm support among the rural plebs, and less so in the city of Rome. Saturninus, who was certainly well aware of that precedent, made sure to rally to Rome scores of supporters from the countryside, both with a view to ensuring their participation in the vote and to use their support in the intense hours that preceded the holding of the *comitia*. The vote in which the law was passed took place after clashes between supporters from the two camps, and in spite of an attempt of the opponents of the bill to postpone the assembly by invoking a religious prohibition. Such controversial circumstances made the need for an oath of loyalty even more pressing from Marius' standpoint, and the issue was promptly tabled in the Senate. At that point Marius set a trap for Metellus and his enemies: his consular office entitled him to speak first, and he stated that he did not intend to take the oath. He fully expected that his statement would persuade Metellus to express the same opinion, and that was indeed the case. When, a few days later, Saturninus raised the issue in a *contio* and called on the senators to take the oath, Marius came forward and stated that he was not prepared to disregard the will of the people and that he would take the oath as stated by the law. For the second time in his career, according to a strand of the tradition, Marius had betrayed Metellus on a matter of crucial political importance.

It was not the only volte-face that he would be making in that political juncture. By that point, according to Plutarch's vivid account, most of the senators grudgingly accepted to take the oath, largely out of fear of the people's reaction. Metellus, however, refused to change his view. That prompted a predictable reaction: Saturninus tried to have him arrested; some of his fellow tribunes reacted to that act, and many inhabitants of the city rose to his defence. Conversely, Saturninus and Glaucia addressed their rural supporters and argued that the land reform would not stand a chance of success unless Metellus was duly punished. They then drafted a decree that interdicted Metellus from fire, water and shelter: the attributes of those who were declared enemies of the city, and were effectively deprived of their citizenship rights. Before the motion was put to a vote,

Metellus chose to leave the city and put the controversy to an end. Although the potential for a violent confrontation was clearly there, he decided not to prompt it. He found refuge in Rhodes, where – as Plutarch admiringly notes – he could pursue his philosophical studies at some leisure. Whether this was a principled choice on his part or a tactical move that postponed the solution of the conflict to a more favourable moment remains uncertain. At any rate, the decree was passed, and a major symbolic blow was inflicted on the hegemony of the senatorial oligarchy.

There was the potential for the beginning of a new political phase. A consul, backed by thousands of veterans, had joined forces with an ambitious and effective tribune to put in place an agrarian reform. Such a remarkable compact of forces had never taken shape to a comparable extent in the late Republican period. Yet, powerful forces remained fiercely opposed to the coalition that had rallied around Marius. The implementation of the agrarian law, which was passed shortly after Metellus' expulsion, knew some significant limits and met with some discontent on the part of the veterans. Marius apparently did not distribute more than fourteen *iugera* (about 3.5 hectares) to each beneficiary of the reform, and responded to his critics by pointing out that the amount of land that he made available was sufficient to secure subsistence levels. The practicalities of the land assignments are largely elusive. There is no evidence that a committee was put in charge of the land assignments, and it appears that Marius took care of them, although no doubt he received expert help. The problem is that the evidence for veteran colonies founded by Marius is at best elusive: there are no conclusive attestations of assignments in North Africa (with the possible exception of Cercina, which played a part in the escape of Marius in 88), and the only foundation for which there is some clear literary evidence is the settlement of Mariana in Corsica.

The main reason for the gaps in our information is the strong emphasis of the literary sources on the conduct of Saturninus and

Glaucia. Marius fades into the background as the initiatives of his associates become more disruptive and assertive. Plutarch describes a farcical scene, in which Marius receives Saturninus and some members of the Senate at the same time, in different parts of his house, and moves back and forth between the two rooms, pretending to be suffering from diarrhoea. Appian's account dispenses with this sort of detail, and goes as far as describing Saturninus' rise almost as an external attack on the Republic, which the tribunes carry out with the crucial support of the gangs of supporters that they could draw from the Italian countryside. The situation became especially tense when the consular elections for 99 BC took place, and Glaucia – by then a former praetor – stood for the most senior office. His rival, C. Memmius, apparently stood a much better chance, and Glaucia and his associates attacked him shortly before the vote was due to take place: he was clubbed to death. The election was suspended, and the city was yet again the scene of a clash between urban and rural gangs. Saturninus and his supporters took control of the Capitol. The Senate declared them public enemies, and instructed the consuls to take whatever action might be needed to address the threat that they were presenting to the *res publica*. Marius was therefore called by a series of traumatic developments to make a choice between individuals with whom he had a strong political connection and the Senate, which was keen to reassert its political authority. He did rally some forces, although it is possible that he was still hopeful for some kind of appeasement at that stage. The dynamics of the riot are not entirely clear: according to Appian, someone blocked the water supply to the Capitol as Marius' troops were getting ready, while Plutarch states that it was Marius' own decision. In a paradoxical twist, the demagogues that had attacked Rome at the helm of a contingent of rural dwellers ended up being besieged in the most prominent sacred site of the city. Saturninus and Glaucia chose to surrender themselves, surely in the hope of being pardoned, or at least spared, by their former associate. Indeed, that appears to have also been the hope of Marius: for that reason he had them locked up in the Senate house, perhaps hoping for the situation to calm down. An angry urban mob, however, took action instead of the consul. In a gesture that was as brutal as symbolically significant, it tore off the tiles of the roof of the Curia, and stoned to death Saturninus, Glaucia and their supporters within the building.

The consequences that this event had for Marius' political standing are obvious. They also marked a new development in the history of political violence in Rome: the outcome of a riot was determined by the initiative of a crowd, against the preferred strategy of the serving consul. According to the version conveyed by Appian, however, Marius had just decided to abandon his former allies and take action against them: according to that version, the old general had just performed one of the many volte-faces of his career. Whatever account one may choose, the events of 100 marked a comprehensive defeat for Marius. The strategy that had led him to join forces with political agitators in order to achieve an agrarian reform failed comprehensively. The reform was not abolished, but there is little evidence that it was implemented to any considerable extent. The extraordinary political capital that he had gathered during the cycle of victorious campaigns in North Africa and Gaul had been squandered. A new strategy had to be devised. By then Marius was in his late fifties, and many will have – ostensibly with good reasons, but mistakenly – written him off.

Elder statesman

The emphasis of much of the ancient tradition on Marius should not make us lose sight of the wider picture: Rome was going through a phase of extraordinary political disruption. Several magistrates had been killed in a riot while they were still holding office; in turn, they had been making ample use of political violence, including the assassination of opponents, to pursue their agendas. Riots had broken out during the elections, the crucial phase in the political process in Republican Rome. The controversial emergency decree of the Senate had again been resorted to. A former consul that was regarded by many as a figure of authority had been sent to exile, while Marius had been allowed to hold the consulship, against any comparable precedent and the spirit (if not the letter) of the law, for several years in a row. In that highly disrupted picture, the personal position of Marius was a detail – albeit a significant one.

It would be hasty, at the same time, to imagine a situation in which the Senate had regained full control of Roman politics. The proposal to recall Metellus from exile was soon tabled, predictably enough, but met with the opposition of a tribune, P. Furius, whom Appian contemptuously labels as the son of a freedman, and who was eventually killed by an angry mob, after leaving office, when he was called to answer for his actions by another tribune. Appian pointedly remarks that not a year went by without some atrocity being perpetrated in Rome. Marius also spoke publicly against the return of his old rival and foe, and concluded that he could not bring himself to witness his triumphal comeback: hence, he decided to leave Rome of his own accord and embarked on a journey to Asia Minor. The reasons that led him to that choice are not apparent. He probably had no previous familiarity with that part of the world (unless he had taken part in the Aristonicus War), although he certainly could rely on valuable connections there. Many members of the equestrian order, where Marius could find much political support and from which he himself hailed, had business interests in that region. It could be speculatively argued that the journey to Asia Minor would afford Marius with the opportunity to foster those political connections. Moreover, during the Cimbrian War his victory had been predicted by the priests of the sanctuary of Mater Magna at Pessinus: whether that response should be seen as evidence for Marius' personal ties with that sanctuary, rather than as an indication of the strong bond it had with Rome, is a different matter. The stated reason for Marius' departure was his intention to pay tribute to the goddess and fulfil a vow that he had made to her during one of his campaigns. Arguably, therefore, it was not just about his own place within the *res publica*, but about the relationship between the city and the goddess. Failing to abide by a vow was a major religious offence, which could prompt dreadful consequences for the whole community. However, it is hard not to see further motives in Marius' decision. The scale of the episodes of political violence that are attested in Rome in this period suggests that he might have found a temporary absence from the city a desirable option, at least in the short term. On the other hand, the view that is more frequently voiced by the ancient sources is that he was coveting a new military endeavour, and set out to trigger insta-bility in Asia Minor and lay the ground for a campaign that would afford him the chance of another military command. Whether this was truly the case is at least doubtful. Much of the literary tradition on this period was heavily shaped by the autobiographical works of Sulla and Rutilius Rufus, an outspoken opponent of Marius. Hindsight might have played a significant role even in the accounts of less hostile authors.

The main argument invoked by those who attributed that intention to Marius is the tale of his meeting with Mithridates VI Eupator, a monarch of Persian descent who ruled over a region that Greek and Latin sources call 'Pontus', in the north of Asia Minor, on the Black Sea coast. From a formal standpoint Mithridates was not on hostile terms with Rome, although he had already emerged as a very active presence in the region, and showed signs of unwillingness to abide by the demands set by Rome. Marius' motives at this juncture are not easy to establish. It is conceivable that he identified Mithridates as the factor that could trigger a regional crisis and prompt a military intervention, of which he might eventually take charge. According to some ancient accounts, he chose to conduct himself in a provocative manner during his meeting with the king, and issued him the stern warning that he should either strive to become stronger than Rome, or follow her orders without questioning them. That the two men did in fact meet and discuss the state of the relations between Rome and Pontus is in itself plausible, even though Marius had no official status. What is far less convincing is the hypothesis that Marius used those very words, which are closely reminiscent of a warning that Alexander the Great had allegedly issued to the Romans in his (almost certainly unhistorical) diplomatic contacts with them.

The motives of Marius in his Eastern mission may be difficult to establish, but it is beyond dispute that his visit should be understood against the backdrop of Rome's increasing interest in the affairs of Asia Minor and in the region neighbouring the province of Asia. The political divides that applied in domestic policy were not necessarily reflected in the handling of provincial matters or in the foreign policy domain. A few years after the visit of Marius, probably in 96, Sulla was assigned the governorship of the province of Cilicia, on the southern coast of Asia Minor. By then he was a former praetor, and he took charge of a military campaign against an associate of Mithridates, Gordius, who was seeking to unseat the king of Cappadocia, Ariobarzanes. His effort was successful in temporarily containing Mithridates' ambitions in Asia Minor. The ambition to restrain a potential threat to Rome's supremacy in the region was shared across the familiar political divides in Rome, regardless of the increasing political and personal hostility between the two men, which was further exacerbated by a remarkable episode a few years later.

Sometime in the late 90s, probably in 91 BC, Bocchus, the Numidian dynast, took the extraordinary step of dedicating a monument on the Capitol, which depicted the scene of Jugurtha's capture by Sulla.

Marius was reportedly furious, as he saw that monument as an attempt on Sulla's part to undermine his credentials, and he started to think about ways of having the monument torn down. Whether Bocchus was directly inspired by Sulla (who had Jugurtha's capture depicted on his signet ring) or was driven by the desire to please both Sulla and the Roman populace (as Plutarch suggests), it was a controversial act, and a memorable one too. Marius' claim over the victory in Numidia was being challenged – and by a foreign ruler. A few decades later, in 56 BC, Sulla's son Faustus minted a coin depicting the scene of Jugurtha's capture, probably echoing the scene depicted on the Bocchus monument (*Roman Republican Coinage* 426/1).

It seems quite clear that, after the end of his journey in Asia Minor, Marius was keen to come back to the political arena. Although his standing was considerably diminished after the events of 100, he could still rely on a degree of political support. During his journey he was elected – *in absentia* – to a place on the augural college, one of the most important priesthoods in Roman public religion. Under a reform passed in 104/103, the *lex Domitia*, the members of the main priestly colleges were elected by a vote of seventeen of the thirty-five tribes, and were no longer co-opted by the priests that were already in post. That election to a lifetime religious office, which also had considerable political significance, is a symptom of Marius' enduring standing in some quarters of Roman public opinion.

Marius' resolve to prove his enduring relevance was confirmed by his decision to move to a house near the Forum, with the openly stated intent to make it easier for his clients and supporters to reach him to pay their respects. As Plutarch notes, this is surely a reflection of the fact that the number of people who visited Marius was smaller than the crowds that others were able to attract to their houses. It is also, however, a symptom of Marius' determination to be seen, and counted, as an important political force. The fragmentary evidence for the political history of this period shows that he still had enemies.

The citizenship grant that he had made to a man from the Umbrian city of Spoletium, T. Matrinius, was challenged in court, albeit unsuccessfully, and Norbanus, one of Marius' associates, was also the target of a prosecution. It was far from uncommon to have politically driven legal actions in this phase of the Republican period, and indeed the series of the criminal cases that were heard by the courts can be used as a reasonably representative chart of the political conflicts and factional divisions across Roman politics. Recognizing that the judiciary system was strongly shaped by narrow and self-serving political concerns does not amount to denying that corruption was a frequent practice across the political elite.

Factional fighting, however, was not the only issue on the political map. The relationship between Rome and Italy was as pressing a problem as ever. In 95 BC, after the census had been carried to completion (the census figure does not survive), a law put forward by the two consuls was passed, the *lex Licinia Mucia*, which had the stated purpose of sanctioning the Italian allies who conducted themselves as Roman citizens, and effectively determined the de-registration of a considerable number of individuals. In 97 and 96 the censors had carried out their customary review of the citizen body and it is possible that they had been more generous in granting enfranchisement than their predecessors, perhaps because many Italians had taken part in the campaign against Teutones and Cimbri. At any rate, it is clear that the law of 95 intended to correct the outcome of the process that had been carried out a few months earlier. The measure was received with predictable hostility across Italy, not least because it was not an isolated incident. It belonged in a longer series of decisions made by the Roman government that had stood in the way of the recognition of the entitlement of the Italian allies to be included – or at least more closely integrated – within the Roman political community.

4

Twists of Fate

The Social War

The tension rose to an even greater extent in the following years. In 91 BC the tribune of the plebs M. Livius Drusus put forward an ambitious set of policies: the enlargement of the Senate to 300 new members recruited from the equestrian order and the handing back of control over the criminal courts from the equestrian order to the enlarged senatorial one. Such a measure was accompanied by proposals that ran against the grain of decades of senatorial consensus: a new plan of land assignments across the peninsula and the extension of the Roman citizenship to the Italian allies. That proposal met with widespread opposition in Rome and, perhaps more surprisingly, among some Italian communities, especially in Etruria and Umbria, where the local elites feared that inclusion into the Roman citizen body would make them liable to suffer from the consequences of an agrarian reform. Most of the Allies, however, backed the measure emphatically. When Drusus' proposals were repealed at the instigation of the consul L. Marcius Philippus and the tribune was killed in October 91, a number of Italian communities decided to take concerted military action. It is unclear how long they had been entertaining such a plan. It is unquestionable, at any rate, that the demise of Drusus played a crucial role in prompting such a traumatic development.

The outbreak of the conflict required a major military response on Rome's part. The option of entrusting the handling of the campaign to the consular pair was not viable: what was required was a complex and wide-ranging military response, on a number of fronts, involving a complex chain of command and the involvement of the best military talents. A situation of unprecedented emergency prompted the return of Marius to a role of considerable prominence: the command of a contingent of troops in central Italy, formally under the leadership of the consul P. Rutilius Lupus, but in fact with a considerable degree of autonomy, partly dictated by the complex geography itself of the conflict. Much as he might have shown some sympathy for the plight of the Italians and the extension of the remit of Roman citizenship in the preceding years, and even more so in the subsequent years, his commitment to the military success of Rome was unreserved.

Not long after the beginning of the campaign, Rutilius and Marius joined forces and faced the enemy by the river Liris, where they confronted an Italian contingent led by Vettius Scato. Rutilius' contingent was attacked by Vettius in an ambush and was partly driven into the river. The consul was struck in the head by a missile and died shortly afterwards. The Roman army was facing comprehensive disaster. According to Appian, the day was saved by a tremendous strategic intuition by Marius, who was quartered at some distance with his own troops, and realized what had happened to Rutilius' troops by seeing the corpses floating downstream. The old commander rose to the challenge and effectively filled the gap that the death of the consul had created. He moved his contingent beyond the river and launched an attack on the Italian camp before Vettius' men could return there. That prevented the enemies from regrouping after his victory, and eventually compelled them to withdraw because of a lack of supplies.

After the funeral of Rutilius, the Senate decided to entrust his army to Marius and to Q. Caepio. Shortly afterwards, when Caepio fell victim to an ambush of the Italian commander Poppaedius Silo, Marius took charge of the whole contingent. In the later phase of the campaign, he even joined forces with his rival Sulla in the operations against the main initiators of the revolt, the Marsians, who were based on the Apennine heartland in central Italy: the crucial engagement with the enemy took place in vineyards, surrounded by a circle of walls, within which the Marsians were chased and massacred. Much of the credit for that action was given to Sulla, who did emerge from the Social War as a major force behind the Roman effort. Plutarch pointedly notes that the comparison between Marius' record in the war and Sulla's did not do the elder statesman any favour. He was by then in his late sixties, and people did notice the different pace at which he conducted the campaign from that of his younger counterpart. Although he did obtain some remarkable victories, it was abundantly clear to many that old age was taking its toll. Here, as in other moments of the biography, there is arguably the trace of a hostile tradition, in which Sulla probably had a prominent place.

Plutarch even states that Marius excused himself from duty in the final part of the campaign, invoking his declining health and his inability to cope with the demands of military life. That was a striking development, especially in light of what occurred in the following months. The Social War was resolved by the concurrent impact of Rome's military offensive and by the willingness of the Roman elite to offer a political settlement to the Italians, and especially to those who were prepared to cease fighting. While the Roman citizenship might not have been the objective of many of those who fought under the Italian standards, that was the fundamental outcome of the conflict. But reconciliation was a long way off. The inclusion of the new citizens into the political system took at least two decades; the human losses had been huge on both sides; and large sectors of the peninsula suffered major material devastations, and faced economic and social disruption for a long time to come. A bitter legacy of mutual distrust and (in some quarters) deep hostility arguably took even longer to fade away.

Disruption and tradition: the first march on Rome

Another indirect consequence of the Social War did not affect just
Italy, but the Greek East, and notably the province of Asia, in western
Asia Minor. In 89 King Mithridates took the opportunity afforded
by Rome's full-scale involvement in Italy to launch an offensive on
the province. Decades of exploitative administration had done little
favour to the standing of Rome among the Greek-speaking communities of the province. In one of the paradoxes that history sometimes
affords, a Persian king was hailed as a liberator by the Greeks of
Asia, and in the space of a few months the Roman hegemony in the
Greek East was practically over. Even Athens declared its allegiance
to the king. The consequences of that sudden, and in many ways
unexpected, turn of events for Rome and Italy were considerable.
Besides stopping the flow of revenues from Asia Minor to Italy, and
therefore posing major problems to the functioning of the Roman
government, it also had wide-ranging repercussions on the economy
of Italy as a whole. Mithridates urged the Greeks of Asia to massacre
all the Roman and Italian residents in the region, who numbered
tens of thousands and were involved in a wide range of financial
activities, from the collection of taxes to long-distance trade. The
violent demise of scores of affluent Italians in the Greek East was a
considerable trauma to the financial stability of Italy. In that troubled
context, there was an urgent need for military action on Rome's part.

The elections for the consulship of the year 88 BC were not just
about choosing the consuls that would oversee the aftermath of the
Social War and the stabilization of the *res publica*: one of the two
senior magistrates was also to be entrusted with the command against
Mithridates. Sulla's record in the war against the Italians had been
outstanding, and his election to the consulship was a predictable
recognition of his recent achievements. His previous familiarity with
the Greek East made him an obvious candidate for the Mithridatic

command, which was indeed allocated to him shortly after he entered office. Sulla could soon start to levy and train the army that he would be leading to the East. The prospect of the campaign was attractive not just because of the significance of the enterprise and of what was at stake for the prospects of the empire. It was also the opportunity to gather considerable war booty: a major set of material rewards that could have proved decisive for the political prospects of the victorious commander (a large array of resources to invest in the Roman political market), and were obviously attractive to the soldiers that would take part in the war.

Against this background, it is unsurprising that others in Rome coveted the Mithridatic command and took steps to remove it from Sulla. What is much more remarkable, and in fact rather puzzling, in light of the portrait sketched by Plutarch, is that Marius took active steps to obtain the command. He was certainly well aware of the political implications of that task, and was probably also persuaded that the war would not present major military difficulties (the development of the campaign was to prove him right in that respect). Whatever his record in the Social War might have been, he clearly felt ready to embark on an overseas campaign as he was approaching his early seventies, in itself a remarkable feat. Equally remarkable is the method that he pursued to secure his aim. He was prepared to follow a route that ran against the grain of established constitutional practice, and challenged the principle of senatorial primacy, especially in matters of foreign policy. A capable and ambitious tribune of the plebs, P. Sulpicius, was prepared to put forward a proposal to the people, whereby the Mithridatic command was to be assigned to Marius. It is certain that the plan had previously been agreed with Marius. According to a strand of the tradition, in fact, Marius offered a wider political deal to Sulpicius: in exchange for the tribune's support to the transfer of the command, he agreed to support Sulpicius' proposal to distribute the new Italian citizens across all the thirty-five electoral districts (*tribus*, 'tribes') in which Roman citizens were assigned. Far from being a technicality, that measure would have enabled the new citizens to have a major impact on the *comitia tributa*, hence on the voting assembly that was chiefly in charge of the law-making process. Its consequences for the functioning of the *res publica* would have been wide-ranging, and many no doubt regarded that project as a thinly veiled attempt on Sulpicius and Marius' part to establish a firm control over the outcome of future elections. The proposal was put forward before the bill on the Mithridatic command entered the public domain, and it did not fail to attract major controversy – Appian points out that the opposition was not between Senate and tribune, but between old and new citizens. Turmoil ensued in Rome; there were again outbreaks of political violence. The situation became so tense that the consuls came to the decision that a vote on the bill was a risk that they could not afford to take, and decreed a *iustitium* – a suspension of public business. That choice fell within the prerogatives of the consuls. It was also, of course, an attempt to stop a project that they both opposed.

It was the beginning of a crisis that had political and constitutional implications, and entailed the wider problem of the balance of power within the *res publica*. Sulpicius saw the margin for a robust intervention, and used his power of veto to declare the suspension of public business illegal. The principle that underlay that choice was strongly asserted: the people had to be given the opportunity to express its view on the bill that had been presented to its attention. The consuls refused to accept the instructions of the tribune, emphatically supported by the Senate, but were soon overwhelmed by the pressure and threats exercised by Sulpicius' supporters. The episode of 100 BC found a re-enactment, but in a very different setup. The consuls found themselves isolated, while the tribune could rely on a wide range of organized, fiercely driven and armed supporters. His associates were not just drawn from the populace, but also included a number of members of the equestrian order.

The fact that the largest army on Italian soil was at a considerable distance from Rome, training in Campania for the forthcoming Mithridatic campaign, must have been a crucial factor in determining that state of affairs. One of the consuls, Q. Pompeius Rufus, fled the city; a close relative of his (a son or a nephew) was killed by Sulpicius' men. Sulla had to find shelter from an angry mob in Marius' house, and had no other option but to negotiate his personal safety directly with his rival. The incident was embarrassing at best. In his autobiography Sulla did not deny that the conversation had taken place, but argued that he had not been compelled to find refuge at Marius, and had chosen to visit him in order to discuss Sulpicius' initiatives and try to secure a solution to the crisis. The exact terms of the agreement that was reached remain a matter for speculation, but two points are abundantly clear: Sulla was allowed to leave unharmed, without being deprived of his office, and he lifted the suspension of public business shortly afterwards. Remarkably, he was allowed to leave the city and join his army in Campania.

This turn of events strongly suggests that the issue of the transfer of the Mithridatic command was not formally on the table yet, and that Sulpicius and Marius had chosen not to challenge Sulla's entitlement to it when he was in the city. It is conceivable that this was a symptom of the balance of forces at the time, and that the stated priority of Sulpicius was to implement a fairer distribution of the new citizens across the tribes. The exact chronology of the events is doubtful: at any rate, it is apparent that the proposal to transfer the command to Marius was put forward and passed shortly afterwards. At a rather advanced age, despite not holding public office, Marius was in charge of a major military campaign. It was an extraordinary turn of events from the days of the riots of Saturninus and Glaucia. It was also a remarkable feat for a man that was approaching old age: Plutarch expands at some length on the somewhat uncomfortable image of Marius doing military training in the Campus Martius along with much younger fellow citizens, looking as keen and vigorous as ever, but showing the signs of a declining body, and attracting an awkward blend of admiration and compassion. (A point is worth making in passing: no portrait of Marius survives, although many were certainly produced in antiquity, and Plutarch could still see one in his own time at Ravenna, in Northern Italy. The busts that have traditionally been identified as depictions of Marius, at the Vatican Museums in Rome and at the Glyptothek in Munich, are portraits of ageing Roman gentlemen who happen to look suitably rustic or austere.)

A remarkable detail recorded by Plutarch suggests that Marius did not envisage the recruitment of a new army, but was expecting a reasonably smooth handover from Sulla to himself: he sent two military tribunes down to Capua to take charge of the troops. He had not reckoned with the reaction of Sulla, the serving consul, who felt he had a legal claim on the command, and had overseen the recruitment of the army that was then under his orders. He decided that the crisis had to be solved by resorting to violence, and that its solution could come from the direct involvement of his army. His consular rank enabled him to address his soldiers with the authoritativeness and conviction that his official status afforded him. Moreover, he had a formidable, if speculative, argument to exploit: he mentioned to his soldiers that Marius might conceivably enlist others, and that they would miss out on the attractive prospect of getting hold of the booty from the Eastern campaign. They had to side with their commander if they were to retain that opportunity. According to Appian, Sulla was initially rather vague on the acts that would be required of them. His soldiers, however, readily understood that the solution that he had in mind was a fully-fledged attack on Rome, and urged him to take action. The military tribunes dispatched by Marius were killed shortly after their arrival.

The army that was about to set off for the Mithridatic campaign was a mighty contingent of six legions, around 35,000 men, and the

decision to march on Rome was a major historical development –
the first one of a series of marches on Rome, which arguably has
its endpoint in October 1922, with the march of Benito Mussolini's
Black Shirts that led to Mussolini's rise to power. It is regrettable
that nothing more than a bare summary of the speech that Sulla
gave to his troops in Nola and of the interaction between him and
his soldiers survives (its accuracy should not of course be taken as a
given). Far from being passive recipients of orders, the Roman armies
in the late Republic were complex organizations, consisting of men
with material interests, individual convictions, overlapping collective
loyalties, and a diverse set of agendas.

The complexity of the moment is revealed by the contrast between
the conduct of the soldiers and that of Sulla's officers: if Appian is
accurate, all of them, save one quaestor (probably L. Licinius Lucullus)
could not bring themselves to march against Rome and the *res publica*,
and deserted Sulla. The army, however, stood by the consul, who also
had, after all, a plausible political and constitutional argument to offer
on his entitlement to the command. This episode is a stark reminder
of the importance of not studying the history of the Republic as the
history of its political establishment. Sulla was met by three embassies
from Rome at close intervals, and pointed out that the aim of his
march towards Rome was setting the city free from tyranny. Once he
was in the vicinity of Rome, he asked to hold talks with Marius and
Sulpicius. They agreed, but did not turn up in person and sent envoys
for preliminary talks, perhaps because they needed more time to agree
on a course of action. The other consul, Pompeius, who had returned
to Rome, greeted him enthusiastically and joined his camp. Sulpicius
and Marius conveyed a request to Sulla to keep his army at least forty
stades (about 7 km) from the city gates. Sulla was quick to disregard
it, and divided his army into five contingents, each dispatched at a
different end of the city. The section of the troops under Sulla's direct
command entered the city from the Esquiline Gate.

As Appian points out, the conduct of Sulla's troops made very clear that they were entering the city as an occupation force. They did encounter some resistance, in spite of the clear imbalance of forces: Marius and Sulpicius rallied a contingent that met Sulla's soldiers on the Esquiline, and apparently the residents of some neighbouring houses also attacked the Sullan soldiers by throwing missiles from the top of the roofs. Marius and Sulpicius ordered the killing of the supporters of Sulla that were in the city, and also made promises of freedom to the slaves that would be prepared to fight on their side: a symptom of their desperation, and a drastic measure that their opponents would exploit well after the end of the conflict. Associating the promise of freedom with a military emergency amounted to potentially undermining the very institution of slavery, and could have (or be portrayed as having) major destabilizing effects. The desperate nature of the offer is further revealed by the apparent reluctance of most slaves to accept it: only three of them, according to Plutarch, joined Marius' ranks. Figures supplied by the ancient sources should always be taken with great caution, but the picture that this piece of evidence is intended to convey is clear. Not even the slaves were prepared to follow the increasingly uncertain leadership of Marius and Sulpicius, and to embrace a cause that appeared to stand no chance of success. The disorder that dominates in Marius' camp is even greater than the disorder that their inconsiderate decision could unleash.

In spite of all the odds, though, the early phase of the clashes proved quite favourable to Marius' forces so much that Sulla felt the need to fight in the front ranks of the army to boost the morale of his men. More importantly, he could rely on a large contingent, and was in a position to call for reinforcements when the energies of the troops that he had led into the city began to falter. When these arrived, Marius and Sulpicius realized that any further resistance was pointless, and fled. Sulla completed the takeover of the city and took over the reins of government, along with his colleague Pompeius. In an address to the people they claimed that they had rescued the city from the demagogues and outlined two measures that were intended to fundamentally redress the balance of power within the *res publica*: no bill was to be put forward to the people without the prior approval of the Senate, and voting on legislation should be entrusted to the *comitia centuriata*, where the wealthier classes were in control, rather than to the *comitia tributa*, where census qualifications did not play any role. They also put forward a number of other proposals, some of which were affecting the powers of the tribunes of the plebs, and saw through the annulment of all the measures taken by Sulpicius after the suspension of public business decreed by the consuls, which Sulla had been compelled to revoke. The legal entitlement of Sulla to the Eastern command was restored; the consul was soon in a position to resume preparations for the campaign and set off for Greece, where he undertook the siege of Athens. He would bring it to successful completion in March 86.

Marius' flight

The march on Rome of 88 was a short-lived episode of civil war. Its aftermath was as bloody as the times that follow internal strife usually are. Marius and Sulpicius had not just lost their political supremacy and escaped from the city; they were also on the run. The Senate had declared them, along with ten other individuals, public enemies, hence effectively depriving them of their civil rights, confiscating their assets, and making their assassination licit. Armed men were sent out of the city to pursue them. Sulpicius was soon captured and killed. Marius, on the contrary, managed to embark on an escape that was soon tinged with the colours of legend.

An extensive section of Plutarch's biography is devoted to this remarkable event. Marius' apparent aim was to leave Italy and cross over to North Africa, a region that he knew well from his involvement in the Jugurthine War, and where he could still rely on a network of supporters, or at least of sympathetic presences. Before he could do that, however, he had to reach a safe point of embarkation on the coast, at some distance from Rome. The most dangerous part of his escape, therefore, was the stretch that had to be covered in Latium. He first moved south-west, heading for his estate near Solonium, about twelve miles from Rome, in the vicinity of Lanuvium, apparently with hardly any escort. His initial destination was Ostia, where a friend had prepared a ship for him; he was also hoping to get supplies from Q. Mucius Scaevola, a distinguished jurist, through his son Marius, who was married to Mucius' granddaughter. Plutarch's lively narrative of the events does not convey a clear sense of their sequence. Marius eventually decided to leave for Ostia and sail off without waiting for his son's arrival; he probably sensed that his enemies were closing on him, and felt that the departure could not be delayed. Indeed, his son came dangerously close to being captured on his mission to Mucius' villa: he was saved only by the help of the overseer of the farm, who – at considerable personal risk, since abetting the escape of a public enemy was a crime – hid him in a wagon loaded with beans, when the horsemen who had been sent to look for him were in the vicinity of the estate. Marius junior was eventually able to flee at night, reach the coast, and board another ship that was heading for Africa.

An escape by sea had of course to rely on favourable winds. It also required an accurate knowledge of the dangers that might be faced on the coast if the ship were compelled to dock because of a looming storm. Marius was determined, for instance, to avoid the port of Tarracina (modern Terracina), about fifty miles south-east of Rome, because he feared the initiatives of a certain Geminius, who was a prominent citizen there and a bitter enemy of his. A storm, however, compelled the ship to land on a beach just as it was sailing near Tarracina. Only with great difficulty did Marius' men manage to find a safe shelter near the promontory of Circeii, apparently at some distance from any inhabited settlement. Plutarch notes that the stormy sea was as hostile to them as the land. Horsemen were patrolling the coastline in search of Marius; moreover, Marius and his companions had almost run out of supplies. As he had done in other crucial – if less bleak – moments of his life, Marius resorted to a prophecy to reinvigorate the morale of his men. He told them that, when he was a child, he had caught in his cloak a falling eagle's nest, in which there were seven fledglings. The seer who was asked by his parents to interpret that sign read it as a premonition of the fact that he would hold the supreme power seven times. To that day, he had held the consulship on six occasions. There was still a future for him.

Marius and his men then resumed their escape, moving south, apparently by land (although it is unclear how they avoided danger at Tarracina). When they were about two miles from Minturnae (Minturno), they saw in the distance a contingent of horsemen that were on the lookout for them; as they turned to look at the sea, they saw two merchant ships sailing along. This moment marks the beginning of the most memorable section of Plutarch's *Life of Marius*, in which the biographer displays his narrative skills. What can be offered here is barely a potted summary of what is, first and foremost, a formidably lively piece of literature, which any student of this period should read, perhaps more because of the pleasure it can give than for what it can reveal about the history of the period. It is immaterial to establish the extent to which Plutarch's narrative has a bearing to historical truth, however defined. From what is a highly charged literary account emerges the extent of the difficulties that Marius faced in the crucial stage of his escape, and the extent to which he came close to losing his life. Plutarch has Marius and his men running to the sea and swimming for their lives towards the merchant ships; it was only with the help of two slaves that Marius, made clumsy by old age, could board the ship, as the horsemen were watching the scene from the coastline, ordering the sailors to surrender him. They refused to hand him over, but were not in a position (or just did not feel able) to shelter him for much longer either, and ended up by treacherously abandoning him on a secluded spot on the coast. By that point, Marius was (so Plutarch says) completely alone: he lay 'speechless on the shore', but eventually started to make his way inland, walking through the marshy land that was typical of that stretch of the Tyrrhenian coastline (until the drainage carried out by the Fascist regime in the 1920s and 1930s). He was briefly offered a shelter for the night by an old man who lived in a hut: Plutarch wonders whether he recognized him as Marius, or just saw in his demeanour a man of superior rank. However, the men of Geminius, Marius' foe from Tarracina, suddenly caught up with Marius, and appeared at the hut: Marius attempted to flee through the marshes, but was soon captured, and was dragged, covered in slime and naked, to Minturnae. The town was a *municipium* – a free-governing community of Roman citizens, with its own magistrates and institutional setup. Although the instructions conveyed by the Roman government could not have been clearer, the magistrates of Minturnae chose to put to the local Senate the issue of what to do with Marius. In the meantime, according to Plutarch, the old statesman was detained at the house of Fannia, a local woman whom he had fined at the end of an adultery case during his sixth consulship, in 100 BC. Marius had reasons to fear her hostility, but the biographer expands at some length on the surprisingly good dealings that he had with her. Plutarch also takes the chance of retelling an omen involving a donkey which, in Marius' view, foretold him a successful escape by sea.

The course of the events seems to contradict that prediction: the Senate of Minturnae sentenced him to death. Strikingly, however, none of the citizens was prepared to carry out the execution. The task had to be entrusted to a Gaul (or a German, according to another source), but not even that foreign executioner could stand the sight of Marius' piercing eyes as he was about to carry out the deed; when the great man asked him, 'Do you dare to slay Gaius Marius?', he rushed out of the room. The story is very dubious, and it should probably be read as an imaginative solution to explain the failure of the inhabitants of Minturnae to execute Marius, which must have been a reasoned political decision. Both Plutarch and Appian stress that the public enemy was allowed to leave the city and continue his escape unscathed. In Appian the sequence of the events is opposite to that set out by Plutarch, as Marius encounters difficulties and dangers on the way from Minturnae to the ship on which he would continue his escape. In Plutarch, on the contrary, the good people of Minturnae, having resolved not to kill him, led him to the sea by the quickest route, even going through the sacred grove of the goddess Marica. The biographer also records the name of the man who offered Marius a ship to continue his flight. Such a zealous intervention in his support can only be explained by the existence of a robust network of *clientelae* of Marius in the area, which not even his status of 'public enemy' could destroy. Marius sailed south; it is unclear who was with him at that stage, although he reportedly crossed paths with some of his supporters at Aenaria (Ischia), an island in the Gulf of Naples. His destination was still North Africa, notably the region around Carthage. He reached it at last, after narrowly avoiding capture as he stopped for supplies in Eryx, in north-west Sicily.

That part of North Africa too, however, was under the jurisdiction of a Roman governor, Sextilius; he was neither an ally nor a foe of Marius, who could therefore hope for his presence to at least be tolerated. To his great dismay, though, he was received by an envoy of the governor, who informed him that Sextilius intended to uphold the decree of the Senate against him. Marius was deeply affected by this unexpected blow, and told the envoy to inform the governor that he had seen Marius as a fugitive, sitting amid the ruins of Carthage. The legendary escape from Italy had failed to come to a felicitous end, and the sight of the city destroyed by the Romans in 146 BC was an apt complement to the disaster which had befallen the former consul. It is a scene of powerful significance, and it is unsurprising that it caught the attention and interest of many readers of Plutarch over the centuries. The painting that is reproduced on the cover of this book, *Marius amid the Ruins of Carthage* (1832), by the American painter John Vanderlyn (1775–1852), is an aspect of the reception of this text and of a deeply fascinating aspect of Marius' biography.

The moment of despair that followed the encounter with the envoy of Sextilius, however, did not mark the end of Marius' prospects. He apparently spent the following weeks on his ship, without being able to dock, while also taking the opportunity to rethink his strategy. His son Marius had reached Africa separately, and succeeded in securing a friendly reception at the court of the king of Numidia, Iampsas, who treated him respectfully, while at the same time preventing him from leaving his court, because he had not quite decided what to do with that inconvenient guest. Only the friendship and support of one of the concubines of Iampsas enabled young Marius to escape and join forces with his father: together they left the African mainland that they had fought so hard to reach and sailed to the island of Cercina (Kerkenna), narrowly avoiding the pursuing king's horsemen: a scene that closely mirrors the narrative of Marius' escape from Italy. The balance between literary fiction and historical reliability is hard to strike, especially for this section of Plutarch's work. The narrative is strongly focused on two individuals, Marius and his son, and on their parallel escapes; Appian, however, also mentions other prominent individuals that joined them on their flight, including Cethegus, Albinovanus, and Laetorius, and conveys the picture of a compact of significant political figures that had left Italy and were now planning to regroup and launch a counter-offensive. Appian is under no illusion about their motives and principles: in his view, they were minded to act just as Sulla had done, but lacked the military capability to do so, and had to wait for the right chance.

The final comeback

The political developments in Rome were soon to afford the opportunity to take action. Sulla left for the East with the army that he had joined after regaining his command; his colleague Pompeius was killed shortly afterwards by the army of Q. Pompeius Strabo, whom he had been instructed to take on by the Senate. The two consuls that had been elected for the year 87, Cn. Octavius and L. Cornelius Cinna, had made an oath to cooperate peacefully before Sulla's departure, but their tenure in office was soon to take a turn for the worse. Cinna's loyalty was with the cause of Marius and his associates, and, even more prominently, with that of the Italians: he revived the scheme for the inclusion of the new citizens across all the tribes, which Sulpicius had put forward in the previous year. The clash between the two consuls soon translated into a new round of violent clashes in Rome, which led to a decree of the Senate that provided for the deposition of Cinna and the appointment of a new consul, L. Cornelius Merula. Cinna left Rome and went to Campania to raise an army, partly relying on Roman forces that were already in the region, and partly on the support of Italian contingents. He then marched towards Rome, where Octavius and Merula had already put in place military defences, and raised troops from Northern Italy and Dalmatia.

It is unclear how Marius caught wind of these developments. He must have been far less isolated than Plutarch would have us believe if he received information on the events that had unfolded in Rome and Italy. His networks of support and patronage in the peninsula were clearly strong enough to enable the flow of valuable political information across a considerable geographical space even at that difficult time. It is conceivable that the connections of the other key individuals of his camp also played a role. It is again impossible to go beyond speculation. What is even more remarkable, however, is the decision that he took once he heard about the actions of Cinna (who should, of course, be viewed as an individual with his autonomous political agenda, and certainly not as an agent of Marius): he rallied his supporters and gathered a cohort of Mauretanian horsemen. Marius' force consisted of no more than a thousand men, according to the most generous estimate, but it was sufficient to give him the opportunity of staging a comeback to frontline politics. It was as bold a gamble as the escape that had taken him to Africa, and the subsequent developments were even more remarkable.

The route of Marius' ship did not aim for the coast of Latium. It went further north, and docked at the port of Telamon (Talamone) in Etruria: Marius might have had reasons to believe that he would find further support in that region, and that the cause of the citizenship reform, which he effectively supported by then, would find backers in that area. Indeed, many local farmers and peasants came to him and offered their support; at the same time, Marius also issued a call to slaves, promising freedom in exchange for their participation in the campaign. It is unclear why he needed to take a measure that echoed the offer made by Sulpicius to the slaves in Rome before Sulla's march if he could rely on the support of large sectors of the free population. The tradition is certainly unsympathetic to Marius and should inspire considerable caution, but two fundamental points seem worth retaining. Shortly after his arrival in Etruria, Marius was again a prominent figure in the coalition that was about to take on Octavius and Merula, and the core of his contingent was not Roman, but Italian, with a significant body of men from North Africa.

Moreover, and most importantly, Marius' intervention showed that the nature of the war had changed in a crucial respect. It was not simply the clash between two consuls, or between a consul and the Senate, over a point concerning political or constitutional matters. It was a war between two factions, which had among their leaders some elected magistrates, but also included private military forces, under the leadership of an individual that, for all his remarkable political record, had no official status whatsoever.

Marius' choice to join Cinna's forces was unproblematic, and was dictated, even more than by any considerations of principle, by the close convergence of interest between the two men. According to Plutarch, Cinna offered him the rank of proconsul – on dubious legal grounds – and the trappings of that office, but Marius made a point of being seen in public in shabby attire, with his hair uncut, displaying the extent of the difficulties he had suffered and his old age. The effect, so the biographer points out, was a disturbing blend of pitiful and terrifying. Yet, the old statesman had retained much of his strategic ability. He also succeeded in winning over the Samnite communities that were still at war with Rome: he offered to accept their requests in exchange for an appeasement and, probably, military support. His impact on the operations was remarkable: since he had gathered a sizeable fleet, he took over the leadership of sea operations at the mouth of the Tiber, while two contingents surrounded the city from the north, under Q. Sertorius, and (probably) from the west, under Cinna and Cn. Papirius Carbo. Marius succeeded in restricting the grain supply of the city by blocking the merchant ships that were heading for the Tyrrhenian coast. He conquered a number of coastal settlements and seized the most important one, Ostia, the port of Rome: the capture of that city gave him the opportunity to gain a sizeable booty for his army. He then moved his forces on the Appian Way and headed for Rome, with a view to joining forces with his allies.

They briefly hesitated on how best to conduct the siege and when to launch their decisive attack on the city. According to Appian, Cinna also attempted to recruit some slaves into his forces by renewing the promise of freedom that had already been made by Sulpicius in 88: on this occasion, it was accepted. The tension of the moment is shown by Plutarch, who argues that the prospect of making the offer of freedom was also debated among the senatorial coalition, but was emphatically rejected by Octavius, who claimed to be firmly committed to the principle of the rule of law. His leadership, however, was increasingly under question, and the Senate started to consider the prospect of holding talks with Cinna: the conditions that he set were the deposition of Merula and his restoration to the consulship. These were accepted by the Senate after some difficult deliberation, when it became apparent that the risk of bloodshed was considerable. Marius apparently emerged as the main threat in that context. During the talks between Cinna and the envoys of the Senate he made a point of standing beside the deposed consul, with a gloomy look that left one in no doubt about how he would have acted if the negotiations had failed.

When Cinna's return was allowed, Marius polemically protested that he would not be entering the city with him, because he was still a public enemy. A decree had to be voted in haste to secure his rehabilitation. The accounts of Appian and Plutarch differ in some important respects. While Appian records the voting of the decree, Plutarch argues that Marius did not even wait for the end of the voting process in the *comitia tributa* and entered the city, surrounded by an escort of armed slaves, whom he had named Bardyaei. It is unclear what the position of Octavius was at this point. In Plutarch's biography, he was dragged from the Rostra and killed before Marius' arrival by some men that had been sent to look for him before the arrival of his enemies, while Appian places his assassination after the arrival of Cinna and Marius, in spite of a commitment that they had made not to harm him. Instead of an isolated and incompetent consul who is treacherously killed before the coming of the enemy, Octavius is here depicted as a magistrate that remains loyal to his office down to the bitter end, and refuses the option of an escape. His head is then brought to Cinna and displayed on the Rostra in the Forum. It was the first instance in which that destiny had befallen a serving consul.

That dreadful act was the beginning of a phase in which political violence was deployed on a massive scale, and a series of massacres unfolded in Rome and Italy. Cinna is widely regarded in the ancient sources as the central figure of that political season, but Marius also played a major part. He took a direct role in the assassination of the orator M. Antonius, who had found shelter in the countryside and was betrayed by the slave of the farmer who was hosting him, and by the innkeeper that had just sold him wine. Plutarch points out that Marius' behaviour was that of an angry man who could not quell his thirst for blood: unlike Cinna, he was willing to take revenge on all those that he felt were slighting him. Ancharius, a former praetor, was killed by the Bardyaei just because he failed to greet Marius when he met him in the street. Q. Lutatius Catulus, the fellow consul of 102 with whom Marius had shared the leadership of the campaign against the Cimbri, was also among the victims: his friends begged Marius to spare him, but they met with a wry refusal. Catulus pre-empted his assassins by committing suicide. L. Cornelius Merula, the priest of Jupiter that had taken up the consulship of Cinna, was prosecuted on preposterous charges, and cut his veins on the way to the trial, but not before taking off the hat (*apex*) that he wore as part of his religious duties: it was forbidden for a priest to wear it at the moment of his death.

What was unleashed after the return of Cinna and Marius was a wholly new way of deploying political violence, and the apt ending to a Civil War that had developed along unprecedented lines: it was a methodical massacre of all the individuals that were believed to be linked to Sulla, or simply opposed to Cinna and Marius. Their bodies were not given proper burial, and were in many cases defaced and decapitated. As the French scholar François Hinard pointed out, those assassinations were not just about the elimination of political opponents: they were also about inflicting on them a 'bad death'. Moreover, they were accompanied by the confiscation of the assets of the victims: far from being a mere set of gruesome retaliations, the massacres of 87 were also the attempt to bring about a transfer of wealth and resources from one sector of the political elite to another. They also marked the end of a political phase and the emergence of a new regime on entirely new premises: the individuals who had played a leading role in Roman politics in the recent past had been defeated in the most public and humiliating form. Their supporters were compelled to share the same destiny. It was also the first instance of a model of political violence that resurfaced in more sustained and radical form five years later, during the proscriptions that followed Sulla's victory in the Civil War, and again in the late 40s, during the triumviral proscriptions. The proscriptions, however, were a considerably more sophisticated process: the massacres took place within a stringent normative framework, under a law that, recognizing them as legal, imposed a set of rules on how they were to be carried out and on how the ensuing confiscations were to be conducted.

The massacres of 87 are generally depicted as a disorderly process, led by the single-minded determination of the victors, in which there is no room for clemency – especially in Marius' case. The sequence of events that unfolds after the victory of Cinna marks the demise of social stability, and even appears to challenge the boundaries of nature. The prominent role that the slave escort of the Bardyaei plays in the events is the gravest symptom of a state of exception that almost appears beyond repair. Marius' decision to recruit and deploy them is denounced in much of the tradition as a symptom of how clouded his mind was in the final part of his life. That monstrous presence was eventually removed from the community itself. The people expressed their deep discontent over the conduct of the Bardyaei, and Marius' key allies, Cinna and Sertorius, ended up taking drastic action: they entered the soldier-slaves' camp and had them killed in their sleep. Marius, however, remained as central a figure in the victorious coalition as he had been since he had joined forces with Cinna before mounting the siege of Rome. Towards the end of the year (devising an accurate chronology of this whole sequence of events is virtually impossible) he was elected to the consulship, and took office on 1 January 86 BC. It was the seventh occasion on which he held the supreme magistracy – an unrivalled achievement in the history of the Republic. He had by then reached the remarkable age of seventy. His colleague in office was L. Cornelius Cinna.

In the meantime, Sulla's campaign in the East was unfolding. Plutarch mistakenly reports that Rome received news that Sulla had won the war against Mithridates, that the Greek East had been regained, and that the victorious commander, still an enemy of the Roman people, was making his way back to Italy with a large contingent of troops. That cannot have been the case: Sulla won the war only three years later, and did not return to Italy until 83 BC. It is unclear whether Plutarch is here uncritically accepting an ancient source or deliberately linking for literary purposes the final days of Marius with the prospect of the victory of his long-standing rival. At any rate, the prospect of Sulla's return may have been viewed as fairly realistic, and another violent clash between two Roman armies on Italian soil must have appeared likely. Appian also points out that shortly after taking office Marius started to make plans against Sulla: he perhaps entertained the plan of recruiting a new army and launching a new Eastern campaign in which he would take on both Sulla and Mithridates – who were both, by that point, enemies of Rome. Plutarch expands at some length on the anxiety and tension that overwhelmed Marius as he awaited the arrival of Sulla: he was in the full knowledge that what he would be facing was a well-organized army, far more capable than the troops mustered by Octavius and Merula a few months earlier. The account that Plutarch conveys, partly relying on the testimony of the Greek intellectual Posidonius, who visited Marius at that time, is disconcerting. Marius was so anxious that he took to drinking heavily to fend off his worries, and was tormented by nightmares that foretold the imminent defeat. Shortly afterwards, his health began to decline dramatically. He probably suffered from a serious form of lung disease, which compelled him to withdraw to bed and he deteriorated within a few days. Another tradition, however, argued that Marius committed suicide. It is fascinating to see that Napoleon, in the remarkable essay on Caesar's campaigns that he dictated at St Helena, accepted it without hesitation: Marius chose death once he had regained the peak of power 'in order to escape the vicissitudes of fate'.

On balance, the version chosen by Plutarch, who bases his account on a wide range of (partly conflicting) traditions, appears preferable, despite its chronological oddities. He relates various episodes that were said to have taken place during Marius' final days: the encounter with Posidonius mentioned above; a conversation with some friends in which he discusses the unreliability of Fortune (one of Plutarch's favourite themes); the delirious state in which he fell shortly before passing away, in which he was heard mentioning the war against Mithridates – the single issue which appeared to be his most bitter regret. Whatever the exact circumstances of his fatal illness and the actual cause of his death might have been, it seems very likely that Marius died of natural causes, in his early seventies, only seventeen days after entering office. He had succeeded in regaining the most senior office in the city after having endured the status of public enemy, but had not had the chance to make a mark during his long-coveted seventh consulship. It was the final paradox of an extraordinary life, which eluded any easy classification and gave the lie to any attempt to reduce complexity to straightforward patterns.

5

Marius' Legacy

The Mariani

The legacy of a complex and highly divisive individual like Marius was never going to be easy to negotiate. It was all the harder to handle in light of the events of the last year of his life: his crucial role in the season of terror that followed the return of Cinna to Rome, and his sudden, premature death early on during his tenure in office. The problem is at the forefront of the concluding section of Plutarch's biography. When Marius died, many in Rome felt that they had set themselves free from a tyrannical regime, only to realize a few days later that an even more energetic despot had taken over his place: his son Marius, who quickly rose to the helm of the coalition, resumed the massacres perpetrated by his father. The task of leading the resistance against Sulla eventually fell to him. However, Marius' place as consul was taken up by L. Valerius Flaccus, who was entrusted with the command of a new contingent of troops to be dispatched to the East, with the twofold task of taking on Mithridates and Sulla. It was an ill-fated campaign, undermined by the disparity of forces between Flaccus and Sulla, and eventually by Flaccus' inability to exercise strong leadership. His legate C. Flavius Fimbria contested his strategy and shrewdly exploited the discontent of the soldiers: Flaccus was killed and then decapitated. Fimbria then embarked on a campaign against Mithridates during which he obtained some remarkable successes. That brief spell was put to an end by the arrival of Sulla in Asia Minor and his peace agreement with Mithridates. Fimbria, who had a strong record of association with Marius, ended up committing suicide, and his troops were installed by Sulla in Asia Minor for several years to come.

Upon his return to Italy in 83 BC, Sulla knew that he would face considerable military opposition. The reassuring messages that he addressed to the Senate and the Italian communities shortly after his arrival did not conceal the reality that a new Civil War was drawing near. The coalition that he faced was a considerably diverse compact, which bore only some resemblance to the forces that had rallied against him and the Senate in 88/87. Although it is often referred to as the coalition of the *Mariani*, it did not set out to continue the legacy of Marius as such: no discernible set of policies was associated with the late statesman. The key ally of Marius in his final comeback, Cinna, was no longer in the picture: he had been killed in 84 by his own soldiers in a mutiny as he was preparing to cross over to Greece with a contingent of troops, with a view to confronting Sulla before his return to Italy. Of course, many men that had fought under Marius were still in active service, and the bonds of patronage (*clientelae*) that he had established throughout Italy, especially as he advocated the cause of the new citizens, were largely transferred to his son Marius, who was by then in his late twenties. His political profile is, on the whole, poorly attested, and his personality as a whole is little known. Intriguingly, however, he is known to have received a formal literary education, unlike his father, and had among his fellow pupils another young man from Arpinum, the future orator M. Tullius Cicero. Whatever his talents might have been, it is certain that young Marius did take up a considerable share of the legacy of his father, and did organize the military forces that would oppose the troops of Sulla. An important role was also played by the consuls of 83, C. Norbanus and L. Cornelius Scipio Asiagenes; Sertorius, who had played an important role in the attack on Rome in 87, was also involved in the operations, before leaving Italy and setting up a virtually independent state in the Iberian peninsula for about a decade. Marius' political weight was further confirmed by his election to the consulship for 82, along with one of Cinna's closest allies, Cn. Papirius Carbo. Remarkably, Marius does not appear to have held any of the junior offices or to have embarked on the traditional *cursus honorum*; he was also considerably below the minimum age for holding the consulship. The strategic choice of the Mariani was to let Sulla march into peninsular Italy on the Via Appia, with a view to confronting him near Capua. The battle near Mount Tifata, however, was a major success for the victor of the Mithridatic War. Marius was in charge of a robust contingent of forces that clashed with Sulla further north, near Sacriportus in Latium (an unlocated settlement in the valley of the Sacco on the Via Latina). He had eighty-five cohorts under his command, and he boldly launched an attack on Sulla's men as they were still busy setting their camp: not even that surprise attack, however, had the better of the enemy. Sulla gave an account of that battle that appears to have heavily influenced Plutarch's account. He also recounted a dream that he had had the night before the battle – one of the many he mentioned in his autobiography – in which the late Marius was warning his own son against the dire outcome of the imminent battle.

The Younger Marius' reaction to the defeat was a hasty escape to the nearby city of Praeneste, where he could still rely on a network of supporters. When he arrived there he found that the city gates were shut (most of his troops had already entered), but he was thrown a rope from the walls and was hauled in. Sulla's troops began a siege of the city shortly afterwards, under the leadership of Lucretius Ofella. A plan was devised by Marius' allies to lift the siege, and the troops of the Lucanian general Lamponius were about to launch the attack, when their attention was diverted by the desire to tackle Sulla near Rome. That confrontation, the battle of the Colline Gate, on 1 November 82, marked the end of the Civil War and the definitive control of Sulla on the Roman political scene. The siege of Praeneste came to its gruesome conclusion shortly afterwards. According to Appian, the crucial step was Sulla's decision to bring to Praeneste the heads of the leaders of the opposite faction that had been killed at the Colline Gate. That sight persuaded the inhabitants of the city that their resistance no longer had any hope of success, and that surrender was the only option. Marius committed suicide just before the end of the siege, after hiding in an underground tunnel. The inhabitants of the city and the Samnites who were in the city were massacred shortly after the conquest, while the Roman citizens were pardoned. A new season of systematic massacres and confiscations, declared legal under a new framework – the so-called proscriptions – was rapidly unfolding, and would lead to an even more chillingly sophisticated development than the deployment of political violence that had unfolded in 87.

The death of Marius' son did not mark the end of Marius' political legacy (quite apart from the attempt of a certain Amatius to claim that he was the son of Marius the Younger, in 45 and 44). That Marius remained a burning problem for Sulla and his associates is strikingly shown by Sulla's attitude to the traces of Marius' achievements in the city of Rome: the trophies that he had dedicated on the Capitol were removed. Any formal and public record of his military contribution to the *res publica* and its defence was wiped out. The extent of the violence of Sulla's reaction, however, stands out most clearly from the extraordinary decision (which one source attributes to his soldiers) to open Marius' grave and exhume his corpse, which was then thrown into the Anio (modern Aniene), a tributary of the Tiber, just north of Rome. A few years later, as his death was approaching, Sulla gave instructions for his body to be cremated, as he wanted to avoid the same destiny that he had decreed for his enemy. The proscriptions led to the confiscation of the assets of the Marii, and to the disap-pearance of their name from the public political discourse for several years to come.

Caesar and Cicero

The sudden re-emergence of the memory of C. Marius was due to the bold and surprising initiative of a young member of a patrician family, C. Julius Caesar (100–44 BC). He was related to Marius through his aunt Iulia, who had been Marius' wife. Since no other male relatives survived, upon her death, in 69, he was entrusted with the task of delivering a eulogy in memory of his late aunt. Caesar had his eyes on a political career; he had narrowly avoided being included on the proscriptions list, and felt that asserting a connection with Marius and his political legacy could serve his political ambitions. He therefore made a point of mentioning Marius and his achievements in the funerary speech for Iulia, stressing her (and therefore his own) connection with a great figure from the recent past, and he made sure to display a portrait of Marius among those of the ancestors of the deceased, according to an established practice at elite funerals in Rome. For the first time since the victory of Sulla – and several years after the death of the dictator – the image of Marius was displayed in public. But there was more: Caesar also oversaw the restoration of the trophies of Marius on the Capitol that had been removed by Sulla, and he took care to do that in an official capacity, when he held the aedileship in 65 BC. The family connection with Marius would also serve Caesar well two decades later, in an altogether different domain, during the campaign that he fought in North Africa against the remnants of Pompeian forces. A number of Numidians and Gaetulians joined his camp when they heard about his connection with Marius, because they felt that their ancestors had been well treated by the Roman commander during the Jugurthine War.

It would be simplistic to label Caesar as a committed advocate of the cause of 'the people' – a *popularis* – even more than it would be to do so for Marius, who had a very complex political trajectory. Marius' legacy could be appealing to many in surprising quarters. When

Catiline (whose first wife, Gratidia, was a niece of Marius) raised a rebel army in 63 BC, he used as a standard a silver eagle that was said to have been used by Marius during the war against the Cimbri: an association that was no doubt intended to confer legitimacy to Catiline's private army, and is nonetheless striking, given that he had had a political connection with Sulla. The figure of Marius also found admirers in political quarters that tended to be emphatically committed to the principle of the authority of the Senate. Cicero, the ambitious young man from Arpinum who had studied rhetoric with Marius the Younger, looked at the seven-times consul as a model and example throughout his remarkable political career. This is somewhat surprising in light of Cicero's political views, but fully explainable with the context of their shared municipal background (they were also distant relatives), with Cicero's status of new man, and with the fact that both he and Marius went through the experience of exile: Cicero was compelled to leave Rome in March 58, albeit not because of the arrival of a hostile army, but because of a vote of the *concilium plebis*, under the proposal of the tribune P. Clodius Pulcher. Although Marius' conduct upon his return could hardly be singled out as a model, Cicero evoked the way in which Marius accepted the exile and the loss of status that it entailed as a model of endurance and dignity. He even devoted to his fellow citizen a poem, the *Marius*, the dating of which is unknown, and the longest fragment of which (thirteen lines) survives through a quote that Cicero included in his work *On Divination*. Marius is there depicted as he correctly interprets an omen, and is singled out for his signal ability to read predictive signs, in a deliberate reference to his membership of the augural college. Cicero's interest in the record of Marius, however, was not just inspired by municipal loyalty or by a sentimental attachment to a remarkable figure of the recent past. Likening his own exile to Marius' entailed a devastating opinion on the nature of Clodius' political action, which was illegitimate even though he resorted to ostensibly legal tools.

In another moment of Cicero's political career, however, Marius could also serve as a valuable precedent: despite his hesitations and inconsistencies, he had chosen to abide by the decree of the Senate against Saturninus and Glaucia and to use his consular powers to secure its enforcement. In early December 63 Cicero did the same in overseeing the execution of five members of Catiline's conspiracy, in compliance with a vote of the Senate. The resort to capital punishment on that occasion was deeply controversial, and was used by Cicero's enemies as the argument in favour of his exile. For him, therefore, referring to Marius was also a way of restating the fact that Cicero's work as a consul was deeply rooted in a legitimate political and constitutional tradition: it served, therefore, some specific, contingent, and very personal concerns. Cicero's assessment of Marius should also be understood within the literary contexts in which it is put forward. In the philosophical work *On Duties*, for instance, the judgement on Marius is considerably more nuanced than on earlier occasions, and the moral criticism of his conduct towards Metellus is unequivocal.

Marius under the Principate

With the end of the Republic the place of Marius shifted from that of political controversy to that of historical memory. He was no longer a model to engage with for the sake of political practice, whether to chastise it or to salvage it from condemnation and oblivion, but as a distinguished figure of the past of the Republic, whose main function was to fulfil a role in the development of Roman history, and who could serve as a formidable opportunity for moral instruction. One notable exception is worth mentioning: Lucan, who wrote an epic poem on the Civil War between Caesar and Pompey in the mid-first century AD, under Nero, evokes Marius in a number of instances, and casts him as a precedent and model for Caesar. The ghosts of Marius and Sulla come back to life at the beginning of the war, and that of Marius resurfaces from the river Anio where the corpse of the great man had been thrown by Sulla's soldiers. In the second book of the poem the extraordinary escape of Marius is evoked, as well as the story of the death that Marius narrowly avoided at Minturnae, when his executioner could not bring himself to carry out the deed.

Lucan understands the age of Marius and Sulla as the prequel of the great conflict that takes centre stage in his poem, through which one may gain a fuller appreciation of what brought about the demise of the Republic. For most of the authors that wrote about Marius in the Imperial period, however, he is a remarkable figure from a distant, if remarkable past; a great military commander, a new man who achieved political prominence, and a model of forbearance before the twists of fortune. This too is how Marius' character is framed in the work of Valerius Maximus, who wrote under the emperor Tiberius and has been mentioned at various junctions of our discussion (not least because of the useful factual information that he provides on several points), and this is how it is codified in the text of the honorary inscription (*elogium*) of Marius that was put on display in the Forum of Augustus in Rome, along with other similar inscriptions devoted to other distinguished figures in Roman history. The focus of that brief text is on two crucial, and yet selective and partial points: on the magistracies that Marius held (with his seven consulships being emphatically mentioned), and on the set of military victories that he obtained and the triumphs that he celebrated. The killing of Saturninus and Glaucia is briefly mentioned as an action that liberated the state from chaos, and the tragic events of 88 and 87 are summarized in a deeply misleading fashion: 'he was expelled from his country through civil strife and was restored through force', the emphasis being placed more on Marius' remarkable age at the time than on the human losses of those years and the political and constitutional clash that marked them.

The final mentions in the surviving part of the text are for the temple of Honos and Virtus that Marius consecrated after the Germanic campaign, and probably for his entrance into the Senate with triumphal robes and patrician shoes. This is a sanitized, and deeply misleading, version of the past, which can be largely falsified by the rest of the tradition, and also a symptom of how the complex story of a problematic figure like Marius could be constructed under a monarchic regime in which there was no longer room for the degree of competition and controversy that had attracted the energies of Marius and many of his contemporaries. The concerns of the new regime are also apparent in the choice of terminology: the expression 'he restored ... the state in turmoil' (*rem pub[licam] turbatam ... uindicauit*), which is applied to Marius' intervention against Saturninus and Glaucia, echoes the expression that Augustus used to define his own actions during and after the Civil War that he fought and won in the 40s and 30s (*Res Gestae* 1.1: *rem publicam a dominatione factionis oppressam in libertatem uindicaui*, 'I restored the state, which was oppressed by the domination of a faction, to freedom'). The fact that Marius received such strong attention under a monarchic and authoritarian power – that he was, in some way, a problem for that regime – is a symptom of his deep interest and enduring significance as a focus of serious and rewarding historical study.

Further Reading

The key literary sources on Marius' life and political agenda are Plutarch's biography, which is paired with that of Pyrrhus, king of Epirus, and the relevant section of the first book of Appian's *Civil Wars*, which is not mainly focused on Marius, but on the whole set of political developments of the period, and has valuable (if sometimes problematic) insights into constitutional, social and even economic issues. The fullest commentaries on these two works are in Italian, and nearly half a century old: E. Valgiglio, *Plutarco. Vita di Mario* (Florence, 1956) and E. Gabba, *Appiani Bellorum Civilium liber primus* (Florence, 1958). T. J. Duff, *Plutarch's Lives: Exploring Virtue and Vice* (Oxford, 2000), 101–30, gives a very informative discussion of the *Life of Marius* and of the role that the theme of ambition plays in that text; see also B. Buszard, 'The Decline of the Roman Republic in *Pyrrhus-Marius*', in L. de Blois et al. (eds), *The Statesman in Plutarch's Works. Volume II: the Statesman in Plutarch's Greek and Roman Lives* (Leiden and Boston, 2005), 281–96, and 'The Decline of Roman Statesmanship in Plutarch's *Pyrrhus-Marius*', *Classical Quarterly* 55 (2005): 481–97.

Sallust's *Jugurthine War* provides a powerful account of Marius' Numidian campaign. There are two recent English editions, with substantial introductions and a full set of notes, by A. J. Woodman with Penguin (2007) and W. Batstone in the Oxford World's Classics series (Oxford, 2010). G. M. Paul, *A Historical Commentary on Sallust's "Bellum Jugurthinum"* (Liverpool, 1984) has a detailed discussion of the value of the text as an historical source.

The books of Livy's historical work in which the age of Marius was discussed are not extant; valuable insights may be gained from the late summaries (known as *Periochae*) that do survive: see H. Hine, 'Livy's

Judgement on Marius', *Liverpool Classical Monthly* 3 (1978): 83–87. What survives of the relevant section of Diodorus Siculus' *Library of History* (books 35–39) provides glimpses of information, but nothing approaching a coherent narrative. There is a brief overview of Marius' life in the *De uiris illustribus* (*On illustrious men*), an anonymous work that certainly dates to the Imperial period: see M. M. Sage, 'The *De viris illustribus*: Chronology and Structure', *Transactions of the American Philological Association* 108 (1978): 217–48 and 'The *De Viris Illustribus*: Authorship and Date', *Hermes* 108 (1980): 83–100.

The fragments of the historical work of P. Rutilius Rufus are edited, with an English translation and a full commentary, by C. J. Smith, in T. J. Cornell (ed.), *The Fragments of the Roman Historians* (Oxford, 2013) no. 21; those of Q. Lutatius Catulus are no. 19 in the same collection.

There is an excellent overview of Marius' life and career by Ernst Badian in S. Hornblower, A. Spawforth and E. Eidinow (eds), *Oxford Classical Dictionary* (Oxford, 2012⁴), 899–900. See also, by the same author, *Foreign Clientelae* (Oxford, 1958), 193–220 and 'Marius and the Nobiles', *Durham University Journal* 36 (1964): 141–54. For a full-scale biographical account in English see T. F. Carney, *A Biography of C. Marius* (Chicago, 1970²); the same scholar also produced a number of studies on specific aspects of Marius' life and career, such as 'The Flight and Exile of Marius', *Greece and Rome* 8 (1961): 98–121 and 'The Picture of Marius in Valerius Maximus', *Rheinisches Museum* 105 (1962): 289–337. P. A. Kildahl, *Caius Marius* (New York, 1968) also provides a useful treatment. R. J. Evans, *Gaius Marius. A Political Biography* (Pretoria, 1994) offers a study of the political history of the late second and early first centuries BC through the detailed analysis of Marius' career; see also his critical assessment of Marius' military ability in *Questioning Reputations. Essays on Nine Roman Republican Politicians* (Pretoria, 2003), 11–35.

There are of course valuable accounts of Marius' career and politics in other languages: K. Weynand, 'C. Marius', in *Realencyclopädie der classischen Altertumswissenschaften*, Supplementband 6 (Stuttgart, 1935): 1363–1425; R. Andreotti, *Cajo Mario* (Gubbio, 1940); A. Passerini, *Studi su Caio Mario* (Milan, 1971: very good on political developments); J. van Ooteghem, *Caius Marius* (Académie Royale de Belgique. Classe des Lettres. Mémoires 56.6, Brussels, 1964: a very comprehensive discussion – arguably the most thorough biography of Marius to date); M. Labitzke, *Marius. Der verleumdete Retter Roms* (Münster, 2013, providing a reliable overview of the ancient evidence). The following bibliography will concentrate predominantly on English-speaking scholarship.

On the political history of the late second century BC see A. W. Lintott, 'Political History, 146–95 B.C.', in *Cambridge Ancient History* IX (Cambridge, 1994²), 40–103, especially 86–103 and C. Steel, *The End of the Roman Republic, 146 to 44 BC. Conquest and Crisis* (Edinburgh, 2013), 26–35.

T. P. Wiseman, *New Men in the Roman Senate, 139 BC–AD 14* (Oxford, 1971) remains essential reading on 'new men' in Republican Rome; see also L. A. Burckhardt, 'The Political Elite of the Roman Republic. Comments on Recent Discussion of the Concepts "Nobilitas" and "Homo Novus"', *Historia* 39 (1990): 77–99. A. Yakobson, 'Marius Speaks to the People: "New Man", Roman Nobility and Roman Political Culture', *Scripta Classica Israelica* 33 (2014): 283–300 provides a thoughtful discussion of how Marius asserted and used his status for political purposes, notably in his bid for the consulship. On the connection with the Metelli see I. Shatzman, 'Scaurus, Marius and the Metelli: a Prosopographical-Factional Case', *Ancient Society* 5 (1974): 197–222; on the political context that led up to Marius' election see G. D. Farney, 'The Fall of the Priest C. Sulpicius Galba and the First Consulship of Marius', *Memoirs of the American Academy in Rome* 42 (1997): 23–37.

The ground-breaking discussions of the scope of Marius' recruitment reform were published by E. Gabba, in Italian, in 1949 and 1951: see the revised English versions in *Republican Rome, the Army, and the Allies* (Berkeley and Los Angeles, 1976), 1–69, 171–214; see also the excellent treatment in P. A. Brunt, *Italian Manpower* (Oxford, 1971), 404–8. A different account in J. W. Rich, 'The Supposed Manpower Shortage of the Later Second Century B.C.', *Historia* 32 (1983): 287–331; see especially 323–9 on Marius' levy and its political background; in Rich's view the enrolment of *proletarii* in 107 remained an isolated incident until the Social War. For more bibliography and a keen discussion of some military aspects see C. A. Matthew, *On the Wings of Eagles. The Reforms of Gaius Marius and the Creation of Rome's First Professional Soldiers* (Newcastle upon Tyne, 2010).

On demographic developments in Republican Italy see the excellent discussions by A. Launaro, *Peasants and Slaves. The Rural Population of Roman Italy (200 BC to AD 100)* (Cambridge, 2011); L. de Ligt, *Peasants, Citizens and Soldiers: Studies in the Demographic History of Roman Italy 225 BC–AD 100* (Cambridge, 2012); and S. Hin, *The Demography of Roman Italy: Population Dynamics in an Ancient Conquest Society (201 BCE–14 CE)* (Cambridge, 2013), which put forward very different accounts of the problem. P. Kay, *Rome's Economic Revolution* (Oxford, 2014) is now essential reading on the economic history of the Republican period (including its demographic facets).

R. T. Ridley, 'L. Cornelius Sulla as untrained master of military science', *Rivista di filologia e di istruzione classica* 138 (2010): 96–115 dispels the view that Sulla joined Marius in Numidia without any military background.

R. Evans, *Fields of Death. Retracing Ancient Battlefields* (Barnsley, 2013), 125–58, offers a valuable overview of the Germanic campaigns of Marius. G. C. Sampson, *The Crisis of Rome. The Jugurthine and Northern Wars and the Rise of Marius* (Barnsley, 2010) discusses the wars in North Africa, Southern Gaul, and Northern Italy as phases of a wider strategic crisis that Rome faced in the last quarter of the second century BC.

F. Noble, 'Dust-clouds, Sunlight, and the (In-)Competent General: Competing Traditions on Marius at Vercellae', *Historia* 65 (2016) disentangles the complexity of the literary tradition on the battle of Vercellae. F. Muccioli, 'Dopo la vittoria dei *Campi Raudii*: Mario terzo fondatore di Roma? (Su Plut., *Mar.* 27, 8–10)', *Atene e Roma* 39 (1994): 192–205 gives a healthily sceptical reading of Plutarch's evidence for the title of 'third founder' of Rome that Marius allegedly received upon his return. P. Assenmaker, *De la victoire au pouvoir. Développement et manifestations de l'idéologie impératoriale à l'époque de Marius à Sylla* (Brussels, 2014), offers an important discussion of Marius' self-representation, closely connecting (and meaningfully contrasting) it with Sulla's strategy – see especially 98–135 ('Marius vir triumphalis').

The temple of Honos and Virtus and its place in Marius' political strategy are discussed by M. McDonnell, *Roman Manliness. Virtus and the Roman Republic* (Cambridge, 2006), 266–92 and A. Clark, *Divine Qualities. Cult and Community in Republican Rome* (Oxford, 2007), 124–30, 156–8. On Marius and prophecies see F. Santangelo, *Divination, Prediction and the End of the Roman Republic* (Cambridge, 2013), 169–70, 186–91.

The evidence for the colonies of Marian veterans is gathered and discussed by Brunt, *Italian Manpower*, 216, 577–80 (Africa), 601 (Corsica).

There is a perceptive discussion of the role that the concept of popular sovereignty appears to play in the policies of Saturninus and Glaucia in D. S. Potter, *Rome in the Ancient World. From Romulus to Justinian* (London, 2014[2]), 121–4. On the circumstances that led to their demise see E. Badian, 'The Death of Saturninus: Studies in Chronology and Prosopography', *Chiron* 14 (1984): 101–47. On the political history of the 90s, see, by the same author,

'Caepio and Norbanus', *Historia* 6 (1957): 318–46 (= *Studies in Greek and Roman History*, Oxford 1964, 34–70).

On Marius' meeting with Mithridates see L. Ballesteros Pastor, 'Marius' Words to Mithridates Eupator (Plut. *Mar.* 31.3)', *Historia* 48 (1999): 506–508.

On the Italian question in the 90s see F. C. Tweedie, 'The *Lex Licinia Mucia* and the *Bellum Italicum*', in S. T. Roselaar (ed.), *Processes of Integration and Identity Formation in the Roman Republic* (Leiden and Boston, 2012), 123–39. On the Social War see the chapter by E. Gabba, 'Rome and Italy: the Social War', in *Cambridge Ancient History* IX (Cambridge, 1994[2]), 104–28; Steel, *End of the Roman Republic*, 35–42, 80–97; and the recent discussion in C. J. Dart, *The Social War, 91 to 88 BCE. A History of the Italian Insurgency against the Roman Republic* (Farnham and Burlington, 2014). H. Mouritsen, *Italian Unification. A Study in Ancient and Modern Historiography* (London, 1998) is essential, if controversial, reading on the motives of the Italians.

The elusive figure of Sulpicius receives a comprehensive discussion in J. Powell, 'The tribune Sulpicius', *Historia* 39 (1990): 446–60. On Marius' position see T. J. Luce, 'Marius and the Mithridatic Command', *Historia* 19 (1970): 161–94. B. M. Levick, 'Sulla's March on Rome in 88 B.C.', *Historia* 3 (1982): 503–508 has an excellent discussion of the political and constitutional considerations that corroborated Sulla's initiative in 88. R. Morstein-Marx, 'Consular Appeals to the Army in 88–87: the Locus of Legitimacy in Late-Republican Rome', in H. Beck, A. Duplá, M. Jehne and F. Pina Polo (eds), *Consuls and Res Publica. Holding High Office in the Roman Republic* (Cambridge, 2011), 259–78 effectively reminds us that the armies that marched on Rome in 88 and 87 were not led by seditious warlords, but by lawfully elected magistrates, and of the implications of this basic fact.

R. Seager, 'Sulla', in *Cambridge Ancient History* IX (Cambridge, 1994[2]), 165–207 provides a valuable discussion of Sulla's political career and agenda. H. Flower, *Roman Republics* (Princeton, 2010), 117–34 is now crucial reading. See A. Keaveney, *Sulla. The Last Republican* (London, 2005) for a biographical account and G. C. Sampson, *The Collapse of Rome. Marius, Sulla and the 1st Civil War (91–70 BC)* (Barnsley, 2013) for a narrative that focuses mainly on military developments. Cf. F. Santangelo, *Sulla, the Elites and the Empire. A Study of Roman Policies in Italy and the Greek East* (Leiden and Boston, 2007) on the proscriptions (78–87) and Sulla's veteran colonization (147–57).

On the place of 'bad death' in late Republican history see F. Hinard, 'La *male* mort', in *Du Châtiment dans la cité* (Rome, 1984), 295–311.

On the age of Cinna see the relevant section of *CAH* IX² and the monographs by H. Bennett, *Cinna and His Times* (Menasha, 1923) and M. Lovano, *The Age of Cinna. Crucible of Late Republican Rome* (Stuttgart, 1999). B. R. Katz, 'Studies on the Period of Cinna and Sulla', *Antiquité Classique* 45 (1976): 497–549 remains useful.

On the Bardyaei see the valuable discussion in C. F. Konrad, *Plutarch's Sertorius. A Historical Commentary* (Chapel Hill, 1994), 71–73.

On Caesar and Marius see L. Canfora, *Julius Caesar. The Life and Times of the People's Dictator* (Berkeley and Los Angeles, 2007), 3–8, 14–16, 89–90 (cf. 341–42 on the 'false Marius') and W. J. Tatum, *Always I am Caesar* (Oxford and Malden, 2008), 33–5. On Cicero's engagement with Marius' legacy see F. Santangelo, 'Cicero and Marius', *Athenaeum* 96 (2008), 597–607 and H. van der Blom, *Cicero's Role Models. The Political Strategy of a Newcomer* (Oxford, 2010). On the ties between the Marii and the Tullii Cicerones see B. Levick, *Catiline* (London, 2015), xiii, 2–4.

On Marius in Lucan see M. L. Delvigo, '*Per transitum tangit historiam*: intersecting developments of Roman identity in Virgil', in J. Farrell and D. Nelis (eds), *Augustan Poetry and the Roman Republic* (Oxford, 2013), 19–39, especially 32–9.

Mommsen's judgement on Marius may be found in Chapter 22 of his monumental *Römische Geschichte* (Engl. trans., *The History of Rome*, III, New York, 1895, especially 261). Machiavelli's *Discorsi* may be read in English translation in the Penguin edition by B. Krick (London, 1983). Montesquieu's *Considérations* are available in the English translation by D. Lowenthal (Indianapolis, 1965). Napoleon's *Précis des guerres de César* is readily available in a number of editions, several of which are open-access, but not in English translation.

J. Vanderlyn's painting of Marius on the ruins of Carthage and Marius' reception in American nineteenth-century culture are discussed in M. Malamud, *Ancient Rome and Modern America* (Oxford and Malden, 2009), 36–39. Another painting inspired by an episode of Marius' life deserves a mention: *Marius at Minturnae*, by the French artist Germain-Jean Drouais (1763–88), depicting the encounter between Marius and the executioner who could not bring himself to commit the deed.

References to the Ancient Sources

Marius' date of birth: Vell. 2.18.6; Plut. *Mar.* 33.1, 41.4, 45.7.

Arpinum receives the Roman citizenship in 188: Livy 38.36.7; Fest. 262 L.; Cic. *Planc.* 20.

Marius' childhood: Plut. *Mar.* 3.1; Sall. *BJ* 63.3.

Lowly origin: Plin. *Nat.* 33.150; Tac. *Hist.* 2.38.3; Cass. Dio F 87.

Equestrian origin: Diod. 34/35.38 (tax-farmer); Vell. 2.11.1; Val. Max. 8.15.7.

Mariani: Plin. *Nat.* 3.63.

Cato the Elder and the study of Greek language and culture: Plin. *Nat.* 29.14; *Vir. Ill.* 47.1; Plut. *Cato Mai.* 2.3–4, 23.

Marius' early setbacks: Val. Max. 6.9.14.

M. Gratidius: Cic. *Brut.* 168; *De Orat.* 1.2.

Plutarch on Marius' names: Plut. *Mar.* 1.

Marii in Italy: *Corpus Inscriptionum Latinarum* 1².1721 (Aeclanum), 1².1575 = 10.4651; Gell. 10.3.3 (Teanum Sidicinum). Q. Marius: M. H. Crawford, *Roman Republican Coinage* (Cambridge, 1974) no. 148.

Marius and Scipio Aemilianus: Plut. *Mar.* 3.2–3.

Sulla's prediction on Caesar: Suet. *DJ* 1.3.

Marius and the military tribunate: Sall. *BJ* 63.5.

The Aristonicus War: Livy *Per.* 59.3–5; Diod. 36.2.26; Strabo 14.1.38; Just. 36.4.6–8; Val. Max. 3.2.12; Eutrop. 4.20.

Tiberius Gracchus and the legacy of Attalus III: Livy *Per.* 58.3–4; Plut. *Tib. Gr.* 14.1–2; *Vir. Ill.* 64.5.

Gaius Gracchus and the province of Asia: Cic. *Verr.* 2.2.6.12; Diod. 35.25; App. *BC* 5.4.

Sallust and the destruction of Carthage: *BC* 10.1; *BJ* 41.2.

Cato the Elder on Carthage: Plut. *Cat. Mai.* 26–27; Flor. 1.31.4–5.

Copies of the *elogium* of Marius: *Inscriptiones Italiae* 13.3, n. 17 and 83; cf. *Corpus Inscriptionum Latinarum* 1², n. XVII and XVIII, p. 195; *Corpus Inscriptionum Latinarum* 11.1831 (from Casamari).

Marius' tribunate and the connection with the Metelli: Plut. *Mar.* 4.1.

Marius' ballot law: Plut. *Mar.* 4.2–3.

Cicero on the secret ballot law: Cic. *Leg.* 3.17.38.

Earlier legislation: Cic. *Leg.* 3.33–35; *Am.* 41; *Sest.* 103; *De or.* 2.170.

Secret ballot on coinage: *Roman Republican Coinage* no. 292/1.

Marius' opposition to a corn law: Plut. *Mar.* 4.4.

Cicero on Marius' electoral defeats: *Planc.* 51; cf. Plut. *Mar.* 5.2.

Sabaco's slave: Plut. *Mar.* 5.3–5.

Expulsion of Sabaco from the Senate: Plut. *Mar.* 5.3.

Marius' praetorship and provincial governorship: Plut. *Mar.* 6.1–2.

Marius and the Spanish mines: Plin. *Nat.* 34.4.

Marriage with Iulia: Plut. *Mar.* 6.2.

The background and early phases of the Jugurthine War: Sall. *BJ* 5–24.

Everything is for sale in Rome: Sall. *BJ* 8.1.

Sallust on Metellus: Sall. *BJ* 45, 64.1–2; cf. Diod. 34/35.38.

Marius' ambitions in Africa: Plut. *Mar.* 7.1.

Lex Mamilia: Sall. *BJ* 40; Cic. *Brut.* 33–34.127–128; *Planc.* 70; *Sest.* 67.140.

Marius at Sicca: Sall. *BJ* 56.4–7.

Turpilius: Plut. *Mar.* 8.1–2; cf. Sall. *BJ* 66.3–4, 67.3, 69.4.

Marius' bid for the consulship: Sall. *BJ* 63–64; Plut. *Mar.* 8.3–5. Cf. Cic. *Off.* 3.79.

Change of mood among the Roman people: Sall. *BJ* 65.4–5.

Marius' election to the consulship: Sall. *BJ* 84.

P. Rupilius as a tax collector: Val. Max. 6.9.8.

Tribunician involvement: Sall. *BJ* 73.5, 7; Plut. *Mar.* 8.5.

Recruitment: Sall. *BJ* 86.1–3; Val. Max. 2.3.1; Plut. *Mar.* 9.1; Gell. 16.10.10; Flor. 1.36.

Clash between consuls and tribunes in 151 BC: Plb. 35.3.7–8; Livy *Per.* 48.12; App. *Ib.* 49.

Marius' speech: Sall. *BJ* 85; cf. Plut. *Mar.* 9.2–4.

Siege of Capsa: Sall. *BJ* 89.4–93.4; Flor. 1.36.

Siege of Muluccha: Sall. *BJ* 93.5–94.

Sulla's arrival: Sall. *BJ* 95. Cf. Val. Max. 6.9.6; Plut. *Sull.* 3.1.

Early contacts with Bocchus: Sall. *BJ* 102.2–103; Plut. *Sull.* 3.2.

Meeting at Utica: Sall. *BJ* 104.

Volux and Sulla: Sall. *BJ* 105.3–107.

Talks between Sulla and Bocchus: Sall. *BJ* 108–111; Plut. *Sull.* 3.2–3.

Bocchus' doubts: Sall. *BJ* 112; Plut. *Sull.* 3.3.

Capture of Jugurtha: Sall. *BJ* 113.4–7; Plut. *Sull.* 3.3.

The city's hopes: Sall. *BJ* 114.4.

Longinus' defeat: Livy *Per.* 65.5; Oros. 5.15.

Caepio's prosecution: Strabo 4.1.13; Just. 32.3.10; Cass. Dio F 90; Oros. 5.15; Cic. *ND* 3.30.74.

Rutilius Rufus restores military discipline: Val. Max. 2.3.2; Front. *Strat.* 4.2.2.

Defeat of Caepio and Mallius at Arausio: Sall. *BJ* 114.1–2; Livy *Per.* 67.2–3; Diod. 36.1; Licinianus, p. 11 Flemisch; Plut. *Mar.* 11.9; Plut. *Luc.* 27.7–8; Cass. Dio F 91.

Jugurtha's death: Livy *Per.* 67.4; Plut. *Mar.* 12.4; Eutrop. 4.27.6; Oros. 5.15.19; Sidon. Apoll. *Epist.* 7.11.

Marius in the Senate after his triumph: Livy *Per.* 67.5; Plut. *Mar.* 12.5. Cf. Sall. *BJ* 114.3.

The assignment of the Gallic campaign to Marius: Cic. *Prov. Cons.* 19; *Man.* 60; Plut. *Mar.* 12.1.

Early stages of the Germanic campaign: Plut. *Mar.* 14.1–3. Cf. *Sert.* 3.2.

Marius and C. Lusius: Plut. *Mar.* 13, 14.3–5. Cf. Cic. *Inv.* 2.124; *Mil.* 9; Val. Max. 6.1.12; Quint. 3.11.14.

Saturninus' first agrarian law: *Vir. Ill.* 73.1.

Saturninus and Marius' re-election: Plut. *Mar.* 14.6–8.

Q. Lutatius Catulus' electoral defeats: Cic. *Planc.* 5.12; *Mur.* 17.36.

The defeat of the Teutones in Celtiberia: Livy *Per.* 67.8.

Marius camps at the mouth of the Rhône: Strabo 4.1.8; Plut. *Mar.* 15.1–3; Oros. 5.16.9.

Martha: Plut. *Mar.* 17.1–3.

The priest from Pessinus: Diod. 36.13; Plut. *Mar.* 17.5–6.

Aquae Sextiae: Livy *Per.* 68.3; Vell. 2.12.4; Plut. *Mar.* 15.4, 18–22; Flor. 1.38.

Election to the fifth consulship: Livy *Per.* 68.4; Plut. *Mar.* 22.3; Cass. Dio F 94.

Catulus' defeat in Cisalpine: Plut. *Mar.* 23.2–6.

Talks between Marius and the Cimbri: Plut. *Mar.* 24.3–4.

The battle of Vercellae: Livy *Per.* 68.5; Vell. 2.12.5; *Vir. Ill.* 67.2; Plut. *Mar.* 25–27.4; Flor. 1.38; Oros. 5.16.

Marius is hailed as third founder of Rome: Plut. *Mar.* 27.5.

Marius shares the triumph with Catulus: Plut. *Mar.* 27.6.

Glaucia: App. BC 1.28; Cic. *Verr.* 1.9.26; *Brut.* 62.224; Plut. *Mar.* 28.5.

Saturninus: Cic. *Sest.* 47.101; Plut. *Mar.* 28.5.

Sixth consulship: Livy *Per.* 69.3; Plut. *Mar.* 28.1–3, 6; Vell. 2.12.6.

Temple of Honos and Virtus: Cic. *Div.* 1.59; Vitr. 3.2.5; Fest. 344 L; *Corpus Inscriptionum Latinarum* 1² p. 195, XVIII.

Marius attacks Metellus: Plut. *Mar.* 28.4.

The soldiers from Camerinum: Plut. *Mar.* 28.3.

Saturninus' second agrarian bill: Livy *Per.* 69.1–2; App. BC 1.29; Plut. *Mar.* 29.1; *Vir. Ill.* 73.5–6.

Marius' public reaction: Plut. *Mar.* 29.2–3.

The assassination of Nonius: Livy *Per.* 69.1; Val. Max. 9.7.3; Flor. 2.4.

L. Equitius: *Vir. Ill.* 73.3–4.

Metellus and the oath: Plut. *Mar.* 29.4–7.

Metellus' exile: Diod. 36.16; Livy *Per.* 69.3–4.

Metellus at Rhodes: Plut. *Mar.* 29.8.

The demise of Saturninus and Glaucia: Cic. *Rab. perd.* 7.20; Livy *Per.* 69.5–6; Val. Max. 3.2.18, 6.3.1; Vell. 2.12.6; *Vir. Ill.* 73.9–12; Plut. *Mar.* 30.3–4; App. BC 1.32–33; Oros. 5.17.5–9.

Metellus' recall: Livy *Per.* 69.7; Plut. *Mar.* 31.1; App. BC 1.33.

Parallel between the words of Marius and those of Alexander: Plut. *Mar.* 33.3; Memnon of Heraclea, F 18.2, Jacoby.

Sulla in Cilicia: Livy *Per.* 76.6; Plut. *Sull.* 5.3–6; *Vir. Ill.* 75.4.

Bocchus' monument: Plut. *Mar.* 32.2; *Sull.* 3.4–4.1, 6.1–2. Cf. *Roman Republican Coinage* no. 426/1.

Marius' augurate: Cic. *ad Brut.* 1.5.3.

Lex Domitia: Cic. *Leg. agr.* 2.7.18; Vell. 2.12.3; Suet. *Nero* 2.1.

Prosecution of T. Matrinius: Cic. *Balb.* 21.48.

Norbanus: Cic. *De or.* 2.89, 107, 124, 167, 188, 199, 203; *Off.* 2.14.49; Val. Max. 9.5.2.

Lex Licinia Mucia: Cic. *Balb.* 24.54; *Off.* 3.47; Ascon. pp. 67–68 Clark.

M. Livius Drusus' citizenship bill: Cic. *Corn.* 1.21; Vell. 2.14; Diod. 37.11–12; App. BC 1.35.

Rutilius and Marius at the Liris: App. BC 1.43.

Battle against the Marsians: App. BC 1.46.

Mithridates' attack on the province of Asia: App. *Mith.* 17–22; Memnon F
22 Jacoby.

The massacre of the Italians in Asia Minor: Cic. *Flac.* 60; Livy *Per.* 78.1; Val.
Max. 9.2.3; Plut. *Sull.* 24.4; App. *Mith.* 22–23; Memnon of Heraclea F 22
Jacoby; Cass. Dio F 109.

Sulla is elected to the consulship: Livy *Per.* 75.7; Plut. *Sull.* 6.10; App. BC 1.51.

Sulpicius' citizenship bill: Livy *Per.* 77.1; Plut. *Sull.* 8.1; App. BC 1.55.

Sulpicius' proposal on the Mithridatic command: Livy *Per.* 77.1; Vell.
2.18.5–6; Plut. *Mar.* 34.1; *Sull.* 8.2; App. BC 1.56.

Iustitium: Plut. *Sull.* 8.3; *Mar.* 35.3; App. BC 1.55.

Sulla finds shelter in Marius' house: Plut. *Sull.* 8.3; *Mar.* 35.3.

Marius' military training in the Campus: Diod. 37.29; Plut. *Mar.* 34.3–5.

Sulla addresses his soldiers: App. BC 1.57.

Only one quaestor keeps his loyalty: App. BC 1.57.

March on Rome: Plut. *Sull.* 9; *Mar.* 35.4.

Talks between Sulla, Marius and Sulpicius: App. BC 1.57.

Promise of freedom to the slaves: Plut. *Mar.* 35.5.

Death of Sulpicius: Livy *Per.* 77.3–4; Plut. *Sull.* 10.1.

Marius' escape: Livy *Per.* 77.6; Diod. 37.29; Vell. 2.19.2–4; Val. Max. 1.5.5,
2.10.6, 8.2.3; *Vir. Ill.* 67.4; Plut. *Mar.* 36–40, *Sull.* 12.8; App. BC 1.61–62;
Oros. 5.19.7–8.

Circeii: Plut. *Mar.* 36.1–2; App. BC 1.61.

Minturnae: Val. Max. 1.5.5, 8.2.3; Licinianus, pp. 15–16 Flemisch; Plut.
Mar. 38–39; App. BC 1.61.

Eryx: Plut. *Mar.* 40.2; Cic. *Verr.* 2.1.113.

By the ruins of Carthage: Vell. 2.19.4; Luc. 2.91–93; Juv. *Sat.* 10.276–82;
Plut. *Mar.* 41.4.

Marius the Younger in North Africa: Plut. *Mar.* 40.5–6.

Cercina: Plut. *Mar.* 40.7.

Death of Q. Pompeius Rufus: App. BC 1.63.

Deposition of Cinna: Livy *Per.* 79.1; Vell. 2.20.2; Plut. *Mar.* 41.1; App. BC
1.64; *Vir. Ill.* 69.2; Flor. 2.9.9; Cass. Dio F 102.

Cinna's reaction: Livy *Per.* 79.2; Vell. 2.20.4; Plut. *Mar.* 41.1; App. BC
1.65–66.

Marius' return to Italy: Plut. *Mar.* 41.2; *Sert.* 5.1–3; App. BC 1.67.

Another promise of freedom to the slaves: Plut. *Mar.* 41.2.

Cinna offers Marius a proconsulship: Plut. *Mar.* 41.3.

Marius and the Samnites: App. BC 1.68.

Rome under siege: App. BC 1.67.

Marius at Ostia: Livy *Per.* 79.4; Licinianus, p. 18 Flemisch; Plut. *Mar.* 42.1; Oros. 5.19.17.

Cinna draws the support of some slaves: App. BC 1.69.

Rehabilitation of Marius: Plut. *Mar.* 43.2.

Bardyaei: Plut. *Mar.* 43.3, 44.6.

Death of Octavius: Plut. *Mar.* 42.4–5; App. BC 1.71.

Death of M. Antonius: Plut. *Mar.* 44.1–4; App. BC 1.72.

Death of Catulus: Diod. 38/39.4.2–3; Plut. *Mar.* 44.5.

Death of Ancharius: Plut. *Mar.* 43.3.

The suicide of Merula: App. BC 1.74.

End of the Bardyaei: Plut. *Mar.* 44.6; *Sert.* 5.7.

Marius' seventh consulship: Livy *Per.* 80.8; Plut. *Mar.* 45.1.

Marius' final days: Plut. *Mar.* 45–46.5. Cf. Cic. *Nat.* 3.81 (*tam feliciter...est mortuus*). Date: Liv. *Per.* 80.8; Flor. 2.9.17.

Marius' suicide: Diod. 37.29.4; *Vir. Ill.* 67.6.

Marius the Younger: Plut. *Mar.* 46.5–6; App. BC 1.87, 88, 90, 92, 94.

Flaccus and Fimbria in the East: Livy *Per.* 83.1–2, 8; Strabo 13.1.27; Vell. 2.24.1; *Vir. Ill.* 70; App. *Mith.* 52–53; Memnon of Heraclea, F 24 Jacoby; Cass. Dio F 104; Oros. 6.2.9.

Peace of Dardanus: Plut. *Sull.* 24; App. *Mith.* 55–58.

Death of Cinna: Livy *Per.* 83.5; Plut. *Pomp.* 5; App. BC 1.77.

Marius the Younger and Cicero: Nep. *Att.* 1.4.

Operations in 83 BC: Livy *Per.* 85; Vell. 2.25; App. BC 1.79–90; Plut. *Sull.* 27–28.

Election to the consulship of 82: Livy *Per.* 86.1; Vell. 2.26.1; App. BC 1.87; *Vir. Ill.* 68.1–2.

Mount Tifata: Plut. *Sull.* 27.4–6; App. BC 1.86.

Sacriportus: Plut. *Sull.* 28.4–7.

Colline Gate Battle: Plut. *Sull.* 29; App. BC 1.89.

Siege of Praeneste: App. BC 1.87–88, 90, 92–94; *Sull.* 28.7, 29.1, 29.8, 32.1.

Exhumation and desecration of Marius' body: Cic. *Leg.* 2.56; Licinianus, p. 33 Flemisch; Val. Max. 9.2.1; Plin. *Nat.* 7.187.

Julius Caesar's eulogy for Iulia: Suet. *DJ* 6.1; Plut. *Caes.* 5.2.

Restoration of the monuments in 65 BC: Vell. 2.43.4; Suet. *DJ* 11.2; Plut. *Caes.* 6.3–4. Cf. Val. Max. 6.9.14.

Caesar, the Numidians and the Gaetulians: *Bell. Afr.* 32.

Gratidia: Sall. *Hist.* 1.45 M.; Sch. Bern. in *Phil.* 2.173.

Catiline and Marius' eagle: Sall. BC 59.3; cf. Cic. *Cat.* 1.24, 2.13.

Cicero's *Marius*: Cic. *Div.* 1.106; *Leg.* 1.1–2. Full edition of the fragments in E. Courtney, *The Fragmentary Latin Poets* (Oxford, 1993), 174–78.

Cicero on Marius: *Balb.* 50; *Rab. Perd.* 30; *Div.* 1.59, 2.137; *Off.* 1.76, 3.79–82.

Marius in Lucan: 1.580–83, 2.67–233. Cf. also Sen. *Epist.* 94.66–67.

A. H. J. Greenidge and A. M. Clay, *Sources for Roman History 133–70 B.C.* (Oxford, 1960²) provide a systematic collection of the evidence for this period; much of that material is available in translation in D. L. Stockton, *From the Gracchi to Sulla. Sources for Roman History, 133–80 B.C.* (London, 1981). M. Dillon and L. Garland, *Ancient Rome: From the Early Republic to the Assassination of Julius Caesar* (London and New York, 2005), 447–80 is also invaluable.

Index